Collins **wild guide**

Whales and Dolphins

Written and photographed by
Mark Carwardine

Collins
An Imprint of HarperCollinsPublishers

**For Mum and Dad—thank you for your endless love,
support. and encouragement.**

ISBN-10: 0-00-720547-3
ISBN-13: 978-0-00-720547-9

ISBN-10: 0-06-085617-3 (in the United States)
ISBN-13: 978-0-06-085617-5
FIRST U.S. EDITION Published in 2006

Color reproduction by Colorscan
Printed and bound by Printing Express

CONTENTS

INTRODUCTION

There is something special about whales, dolphins, and porpoises. They are still shrouded in mystery, yet the little we do know about them is both astonishing and awe-inspiring. They include the largest animal on Earth, the deepest-diving mammal, the mammal with the longest known migration, species that are capable of emitting the loudest sounds in nature, and many other extraordinary creatures. They also include some of the world's most critically endangered species.

Watching them in the wild is probably the ultimate wildlife experience. Once you have met a whale, dolphin, or porpoise face to face, life is never exactly the same again. There is an immense and lasting satisfaction in simply knowing that it is out there, wild and free. Who could ever forget the sight of a 50-ton southern right whale launching itself high into the air, or of a sperm whale diving into the cold, dark depths hundreds or even thousands of feet below the surface? Who could fail to be intrigued by

Short-beaked common dolphin, Sea of Cortez, Mexico

Southern right whales, Western Cape, South Africa

Bahamonde's beaked whale, which is known from only two partial skulls, an old tooth, and a lower jaw, or remain untouched by the plight of the last few surviving Yangtze river dolphins?

It is not surprising that every year more than 10 million people join organized trips to watch whales and dolphins, in at least 87 different countries and overseas territories around the world.

The aim of this book is to introduce the world of whales, dolphins, and porpoises and to provide a handy pocket guide for use in the field. It includes information on their evolution, biology, and natural history, describes how they are studied, the threats they face, and some of the efforts to protect the ones most in trouble. But most of all it provides a comprehensive directory of all 84 species currently recognized—and a few more that could become distinct species in the future. I hope it will help you to find, recognize, watch, enjoy, and respect whales, dolphins, and porpoises in the wild.

THE NATURAL HISTORY OF WHALES, DOLPHINS, AND PORPOISES

Evolution

The broad outline of the evolution of whales, dolphins, and porpoises is very well known, but there are still many gaps in our knowledge. Tiny fragments—a few teeth or miniscule pieces of bone—sometimes provide the only tantalizing clues to important links in their evolutionary chain.

They are believed to have evolved from a group of furry land mammals called mesonychids. These strange creatures looked somewhat like wolves, with four legs and a tail, but had hooves—so whales and hoofed animals such as hippos and deer appear to have a common ancestor. They lived around the ancient Tethys Sea, an area that is now the Mediterranean Sea and part of the Asian subcontinent, about 55–60 million years ago. The mesonychids probably

Mesonychid

spent their lives foraging for fish and other aquatic animals in coastal swamps and estuaries. As they spent more and more time in the water their bodies began to change. They became more streamlined and developed powerful, flattened tails; their forelimbs gradually turned into paddles and their hindlimbs wasted away; they developed insulating layers of fat and their body hair began to disappear; and, to help them breathe at the surface, their nostrils started to move toward the top of their heads to become blowholes.

It is still possible to see evidence of these land-based ancestors in modern whales, dolphins, and porpoises. Intriguingly, the bone structure of the pectoral fin, or flipper, closely resembles an arm and hand with fingers; and, trapped inside the blubber, are the remains of pelvic bones that millions of years ago held their hindlimbs.

The first real whalelike animals appeared about 10 million years later. These ancient whales, or archeocetes, spread rapidly throughout the oceans of the world—their fossilized remains have been found as far afield as Britain, Canada, Australia, and even Antarctica. They were probably very similar to modern whales, dolphins, and porpoises, although they were less well adapted to life in the sea. They may even have clambered back onto land to breed, just like modern seals.

For reasons that are unclear the last of the archeocetes probably died out about 25–30 million years ago but, by this time, representatives of more modern whales, dolphins, and porpoises were fairly common and widespread. None were exactly the same as the species alive today, but they were unmistakably similar in appearance and way of life. The split between toothed whales (odontocetes) and baleen whales (mysticetes) occurred some 25–35 million years ago and by about five million years ago most, if not all, modern families of whales, dolphins and porpoises had become firmly established.

Archeocete

Diversity

The sheer diversity of whales, dolphins, and porpoises tends to surprise many people. A few species, such as the killer whale, narwhal, and bottlenose dolphin, are relatively well known. But the vast majority go unnoticed by all but the most dedicated whale-watchers.

In fact, there are currently no fewer than 84 recognized species altogether and, as research progresses, new discoveries continue to be made and the total count slowly but surely increases. A new species of beaked whale, Perrin's beaked whale, was formally recognized as recently as 2002 and the latest genetic research is revealing that some animals previously thought to be single species should actually be "split." In 1995, for example, the common dolphin was officially separated into two distinct species, now known as the short-beaked common dolphin and the long-beaked common dolphin. In the late 1990s, the minke whale was split into the common minke and the Antarctic minke and, in the future, it is possible that a third species—the dwarf minke—could be declared.

There is also some debate about Bryde's whales. A pygmy form will likely be assigned separate species status in the near future and, according to recent evidence from Japan, a third species is also possible. In the late 1970s, eight unidentified

Spinner dolphin, The Maldives

baleen whales were caught in the Indo-Pacific by Japanese whalers—and, in 1998, a ninth specimen was found beached on an island in the Sea of Japan. They all resembled fin whales, but were much smaller and had slightly unusual skulls and a different number of baleen plates. Genetic studies group all nine animals together as a single species, but separate them from all known baleen whale species.

While all these animals share many characteristics, there is no "typical" whale, dolphin, or porpoise. In size alone, they range from tiny dolphins and porpoises just over three feet long, to whales that are known to reach lengths of more than 110 feet. In terms of weight, the heaviest species is no less than 3,000 times heavier than the lightest.

They abound in an amazing variety of different shapes as well. Some are long and slender, others short and stocky. Some have huge dorsal fins, others have no fins at all. Many are brightly colored or striking in black and white, while others are somewhat drab.

They also have a range of different habits and lifestyles. Some live in freezing cold waters near the poles, others prefer the warmer waters of the tropics. Many live in the middle of the deepest oceans, but others prefer to be much closer to shore, while a few even live hundreds of miles inland in rivers such as the Yangtze, the Ganges, and the Amazon.

Humpback whale, Monterey Bay, USA

Is it a whale, a dolphin, or a porpoise?

Whales, dolphins, and porpoises are known collectively as cetaceans. They form the largest of the three main groups of marine mammals surviving today, the others being the pinnipeds (seals, sea lions, and walrus) and the sirenians (sea cows or manatees and dugong).

Interestingly, there is no real scientific basis for splitting cetaceans into the three groups commonly known as "whales," "dolphins," and "porpoises." Broadly speaking, the word "whale" is used to describe the largest animals, "dolphin" to describe the medium-sized ones, and "porpoise" to describe the smallest. But this can be misleading, since some whales are smaller than the largest dolphins, and some dolphins are smaller than the largest porpoises.

There are many more confusing names and terms, as well. The rightwhale dolphins, for example, were named after right whales but are actually dolphins. At the same time, many are known by umpteen different names in at least as many different languages. Thus the northern giant bottlenose whale, North Pacific bottlenose whale, giant four-toothed whale, northern four-toothed whale, and Baird's

Melon-headed whales, The Maldives

beaked whale are all the same species.

Even more confusing are six members of the dolphin family, the Delphinidae, which have the word "whale" in their names: killer whale, pygmy killer whale, false killer whale, melon-headed whale, long-finned pilot whale, and short-finned pilot whale. These six species are often classified together in a group known as the "blackfish," which is also rather strange since not all of them are black and, of course, none is a fish.

Scientists prefer to split modern cetaceans into just two distinct groups: the toothed whales, or Odontocetes, and the baleen whales, or Mysticetes. There was also a third group, known as the ancient whales or Archeocetes, but all its members have been extinct for millions of years.

As their name suggests, the toothed whales possess teeth; this group of 71 species includes all the beaked whales, sperm whales, blackfish, oceanic dolphins, river dolphins, and porpoises. The baleen whales make up the remaining 13 species and, instead of teeth, have hundreds of strange-looking baleen plates hanging down from their upper jaws; they make up for their lack of numbers by including most of the larger and better-known whales, including the blue, humpback, gray, and right whales.

Inside and out

Whales, dolphins, and porpoises are so streamlined, and so well adapted to life underwater, that they look somewhat like sharks and other large fish. They even have similar dorsal fins, flippers, and powerful tails. But appearances can be deceptive. The similarities between them are simply the result of two unrelated groups of animals adapting in similar ways to identical living conditions. On closer inspection, there are actually more differences between them than there are similarities.

In particular, fish are cold-blooded, use their gills to extract all the oxygen they need directly from the water, and normally lay eggs or give birth to young that can feed themselves. In contrast, whales, dolphins, and porpoises are mammals, like us, and so are warm-blooded, breathe air with lungs, and give birth to young that feed on their

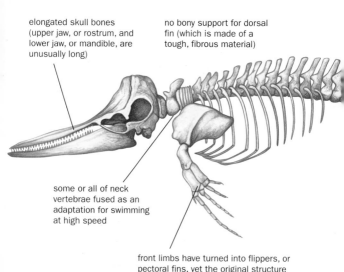

elongated skull bones
(upper jaw, or rostrum, and
lower jaw, or mandible, are
unusually long)

no bony support for dorsal
fin (which is made of a
tough, fibrous material)

some or all of neck
vertebrae fused as an
adaptation for swimming
at high speed

front limbs have turned into flippers, or
pectoral fins, yet the original structure
of the bones of the arm, hand, and
fingers is still visible

mother's milk for the first weeks or months of life.

One of the most striking features of any cetacean is the thick layer of insulating fat under the skin, known as blubber, which they have instead of hair or fur. This helps them to keep warm in water, which sucks heat out of a mammal up to 25 times faster than in air.

A detailed look inside their bodies reveals many other interesting features and adaptations for their underwater life:

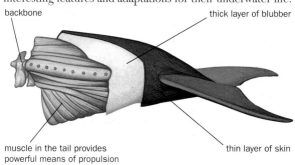

backbone

thick layer of blubber

muscle in the tail provides powerful means of propulsion

thin layer of skin

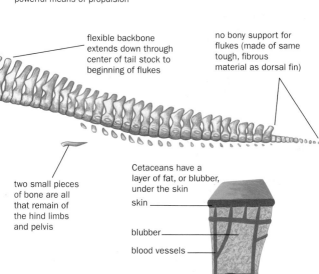

flexible backbone extends down through center of tail stock to beginning of flukes

no bony support for flukes (made of same tough, fibrous material as dorsal fin)

two small pieces of bone are all that remain of the hind limbs and pelvis

Cetaceans have a layer of fat, or blubber, under the skin

skin

blubber

blood vessels

muscles

Diving and swimming

The fastest speed ever achieved by a human swimmer is an incredible 5.37 mph by American Tom Jager, on March 23, 1990, in Nashville. Equally impressive, the record depth attained for no-limits freediving is 686 feet; achieved by Belgian, Patrick Musimu on June 30, 2005, in the Red Sea.

But these superhuman feats barely register on the scale of the swimming and diving records achieved by whales, dolphins, and porpoises. Killer whales, Dall's porpoises and several other species have been clocked at speeds of up to 34 mph, while sperm whales (and, possibly, some beaked whales) can dive to depths of at least 6,560 feet and have been known to stay underwater for nearly two hours at a time.

All cetaceans are proficient swimmers and divers, even though they breathe air and, consequently, have to hold their breath whenever they disappear underwater. Their lungs are relatively small, but they are able to extract much more oxygen from the air than human lungs and then use it far more efficiently.

Killer whales, Monterey Bay, western USA

Avoiding the "bends": Human scuba divers can suffer from a potentially fatal condition known as decompression sickness, or the "bends." It is caused by nitrogen bubbling out of the blood, either when the divers stay down for too long or when they rise to the surface too quickly. These bubbles then lodge in joints and cause severe pain, or in vital blood vessels and cause paralysis or even death.

Marine biologists have always assumed that cetaceans are immune to the bends, but now it seems that rising to the surface too quickly from deep water may be just as dangerous for them as it is for us. Damage consistent with decompression sickness has been found in the bones of sperm whales and beaked whales.

Humpback whale, Silver Bank, Dominican Republic

Avoiding "nitrogen narcosis": On deep dives, human scuba divers can suffer from another dangerous condition called "nitrogen narcosis." They start losing control over what they are doing and their judgement begins to deteriorate, as if they are drunk. In a way, they behave like car drivers under the influence of alcohol because, although nitrogen narcosis is not dangerous in itself, it makes accidents far more likely.

Whales, dolphins, and porpoises do not suffer from nitrogen narcosis because it is induced by breathing nitrogen under pressure and they breathe it in only at the surface.

Food and feeding

Most whales, dolphins, and porpoises feed on fish, squid, or crustaceans, but some will take a wide variety of other prey as well—at virtually every level in the marine ecosystem—ranging from octopuses to other large whales.

Between them, they have an astonishing range of different hunting techniques. For example, killer whales in Patagonia will beach themselves to catch sea lion pups; strap-toothed whales suck squid into their mouths so quickly that the squid appear to have been attached to pieces of invisible elastic; belugas blast powerful jets of water to dislodge fish hiding in mud on the seabed; dolphins of the open ocean work together to corral fish against the surface of the sea; and blue whales take huge quantities of water into their mouths, and then filter out as much as four tons of shrimplike krill every day.

In turn, they themselves are preyed upon by large sharks and even by some of their own kind: killer whales, false killer whales, and pygmy killer whales. The smaller species are most at risk, but no whale is too large for a determined pod of killer whales.

Teeth: As their name suggests, all toothed whales have teeth. But the number varies greatly from species to species and, in some female beaked whales, they have no visible teeth at all (they do not erupt). Cetacean teeth come in a variety of shapes and sizes, but in most cases each species has just one design—in other words, they are not differentiated into incisors, canines, premolars, and molars. Unlike other mammals, toothed whales do not have two sets of teeth, but retain their first set for life.

Sperm whale   Ginkgo-toothed   Fraser's
beaked whale   dolphin

Baleen plates: Instead of teeth, most large whales have hundreds of strange-looking structures hanging down from their upper jaws. These are called baleen plates. They overlap one another, inside the mouth, to form bristly sieves for filtering small animals out of the seawater. Some 400–700 baleen plates is typical for most whales, but their number, size and shape varies greatly from species to species.

Bowhead   Fin   Minke

Krill: Krill are small, shrimplike crustaceans, known in the scientific world as euphausiids. Full of protein, and living in dense swarms, they make ideal food for large whales. There are at least 80 different species of krill, ranging in length from ⅛ inch to just over two inches, but perhaps the most important is the Antarctic krill at 2–2 ¼ inches in length. This is the staple food of all baleen whales in the Antarctic, which also eat fish, squid, penguins, and seals.

Migration

Many large baleen whales have little choice but to split their year into four distinct parts. They spend a few months, in the summer, gorging themselves on schooling fish and krill, in high-latitude, cold-water feeding grounds; in the fall, they migrate to low-latitude, warm-water breeding grounds; then they spend a few months during the winter mating and calving; and finally, in the spring, they migrate all the way back to their feeding grounds, and the annual cycle begins all over again.

The problem they face is that most of their food is in colder regions, in temperate latitudes, and toward the subarctic and the Antarctic. In an ideal world, this is where they would live all year. Unfortunately, though, the food is only present in large quantities during the summer and, even if they stayed for the winter to breed, their newborn calves may not be able to survive the freezing cold temperatures. In other words, their preferred feeding and breeding grounds can be thousands of miles apart.

Short-finned pilot whale, western USA

Researchers studying whale migration have made some incredible discoveries in recent years. Some humpback whales, for example, swim between their feeding grounds near the Antarctic Peninsula and their breeding grounds off the coast of Colombia every year—an astonishing round-trip of some 11,000 miles. Another humpback whale was recorded swimming all the way across the North Pacific, from southeast Alaska to Hawaii, in just 39 days.

But in most cases the more subtle details of their migrations are still a mystery. How do they know when to leave, and when to return? How do they find their way? Do they stop to rest, or feed? Do they swim near the surface, or travel at depth? There are so many unanswered questions.

Not all large baleen whales undertake these extensive migrations. Many Bryde's and minke whales are able to live in nonextreme temperatures all year, while sei whales, and some humpbacks and grays, do not bother to complete their journeys if they find adequate food supplies en route. Fin whales in Mexico's Sea of Cortez, and blue whales in the northern Indian Ocean, seem to be permanent residents, while bowhead whales simply move backward and forward in their high Arctic home, with the advancing and retreating ice.

Regular long-distance migrations are virtually unknown in toothed whales, with one major exception. While female and young sperm whales spend most of their lives in warm waters, many of the older males are believed to move to rich feeding grounds, in high-latitude cold waters, during the spring and summer.

Blue whale, Sea of Cortez, Mexico

Reproduction and social life

There are almost as many different reproductive strategies and ways of living together as there are species of whales, dolphins, and porpoises. But it is a difficult field of research, and we are only just beginning to learn about the private lives of some better-known species.

Sexual maturity: The age of sexual maturity varies greatly from species to species. At one extreme, male sperm whales are not sexually mature until they are about 18–21 years old; even then, they often have to wait another few years before they are big and strong enough to gain access to receptive females. At the other extreme, female harbor porpoises reach sexual maturity at about three years of age and begin to breed the following year. After reaching breeding age, the females of many species spend their entire adult lives either with a calf by their side or a fetus growing inside them—or both.

Blue whale mother and calf, Sea of Cortez, Mexico

Courtship and mating: Courtship and mating can be long and involved affairs, with leaping, games of chase, and touching and caressing taking place for several hours before the two animals join together, belly to belly, though the details vary greatly from one species to another. In some species, such as humpback whales, there can be intense competition and serious fighting between males battling over access to females. There are no records of cetaceans being monogamous—it has never been known for one male to mate exclusively with one female. In the sperm whale, beaked whales, and some other species, one male mates with many females; but, in most species, they are believed to be promiscuous: each individual mates with numerous other individuals of the opposite sex.

Gestation period: The gestation period is unknown for many cetaceans, but seems to range from about eight months in some porpoises to at least 16 months in sperm whales; there is a possible record of 18 months 28 days for one particular sperm whale. Surprisingly, it is not dependent on body size: in the blue whale, for example, it is roughly 11–12 months, whereas in the much smaller narwhal it is at least 14 months.

Birth: Few cetacean births have been witnessed in captivity, and even fewer in the wild, but we are gradually building up a reasonable picture of what happens. Like most mammals, whales, dolphins, and porpoises give birth to live young, although they normally have just one at a time. The calves are born underwater, near the surface where it is easier for them to catch their first breath, and their eyes are already open. They are able to swim, albeit a little awkwardly, almost as soon as they enter the water. The calves are virtually identical to their parents, although their dorsal fins and tail flukes are more rubbery and they do not have baleen or teeth (which begin to erupt when they are a few weeks old). They are normally about one-third of the length of their mothers. A newborn blue whale, for example, is an incredible 23 feet long and weighs some three tons in total.

Nursing: It is believed that the father plays no active role in caring for the calf, so it is the mother's responsibility alone. Suckling takes place underwater, and she literally squirts her rich, fat-laden milk into the young animal's mouth. The calf grows quickly. A young blue whale, for example, grows almost two inches and gains 198 pounds every day—equivalent to the weight of an average adult man. Weaning is usually gradual, with a period of overlap when the calf is drinking milk and eating solid food at the same time. It stays with its mother for weeks, months, or even years afterward, depending on the species. In general, toothed whales tend to have fewer young and look after them for a relatively long time, whereas baleen whales have more young and look after them for a relatively short time.

Lifespan: It is difficult to assess the ages of whales, dolphins, and porpoises accurately and the maximum lifespan for most species is unknown. However, the limited information available suggests that the larger whales tend to have the longest lifespans—probably well in excess of 100 years in the bowhead whale and some others. Certain dolphins and porpoises may have an average life expectancy of less than 20 years. The two main natural causes of death are predation and disease. A variety of accidents and, of course, human-induced deaths also take their toll.

Social life: Whales, dolphins, and porpoises often have complex social lives and have adopted many different ways of living together. Some prefer to live alone, or in small groups, while others roam the seas in the company of hundreds or thousands of their contemporaries. Historically, there are even records of dolphin schools at least 100,000 strong. Some species, such as killer whales and long-finned pilot whales, live in groups that are stable for many years—they remain together for the entire lives of the individuals in them. Others are incredibly fluid and their membership changes all the time, with individuals coming and going quite freely. Often, the membership of a group will vary according to specific requirements on a day-by-day or even hour-by-hour basis.

Commonly asked questions

How intelligent are they?

Are whales, dolphins, and porpoises as intelligent as we would like to believe? They certainly *seem* to be intelligent: they have large brains, frequently live in complex societies, help one another in times of trouble, learn from experience, are often playful, and sometimes even seem to enjoy human company. But, in truth, no one really knows. Some people claim that they are no more intelligent than cats and dogs, while others go so far as to say that they may be our intellectual superiors.

There are two main reasons for this confusion. The first lies in defining what we mean by "intelligent" and then taking meaningful measurements. Many definitions have been proposed over the years, but intelligence is broadly considered to be an ability to learn from experience and then to analyze new situations, rather than simply reacting

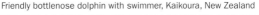

Friendly bottlenose dolphin with swimmer, Kaikoura, New Zealand

to them. In other words, intelligent animals are able to *solve* problems by grasping fundamental principles, and then making considered judgements, rather than fumbling around trying to get things right by trial and error. Even with an acceptable definition, though, obtaining accurate measurements is another matter altogether. It is hard enough in humans, because the results can be frustratingly ambiguous and difficult to understand. But it is even more challenging in other animals that cannot talk or work with tools such as pens or computers.

The second reason is that any discussion of intelligence tends to be highly subjective. After all, we have only a human perspective, and can scarcely imagine what goes on inside another animal's mind. Even by saying that a whale or dolphin is more intelligent than, say, a rat or a chicken, we impose a very egocentric set of values and rules.

The simple fact that whales, dolphins, and porpoises have embarked on a completely different evolutionary path from our own makes any comparison almost impossible. Human intelligence suits our own way of life and, consequently, a large part of our brain deals with the use of hands to write, paint, sculpt, build, or manipulate objects that exist outside our own bodies.

If we were to judge whales and dolphins on these terms, they would fare badly. But their intelligence suits a completely different way of life, and may concentrate instead on social skills, emotional self-control, and other more spiritual and philosophical requirements. Taking this into consideration, many people would argue that whales and dolphins are far more intelligent in their world than we are in ours. But the jury is still out on that question.

Why do they strand?

Every year, hundreds or even thousands of whales, dolphins, and porpoises are found stranded on coastlines all over the world. They may be alive or dead, alone or in groups, and healthy or unwell. These strandings are believed to be a natural phenomenon (although, in modern times, pollution and acoustic disturbance may be contributory causes in some areas) and have probably been happening for thousands of years. But *why* they happen remains one of the great unsolved mysteries of the animal kingdom.

Strandings of dead animals are relatively easy to explain—they simply die at sea and are washed ashore with the tides and currents—and live animals often strand because they are very ill. But mass strandings of otherwise healthy animals are more baffling. Many theories have been suggested, ranging from severe weather (quite possible) to mass suicide bids (highly unlikely).

But recent research implies that it could be storms exploding from the Sun that are making the whales run aground. Historical records of sperm whales found beached in the North Sea, over a 300-year period, show an amazing match with the number of "sunspots" that blast electrical energy into space. This smashes into the Earth's magnetic field (which the whales may use for navigation) and disrupts their internal compasses.

In reality, of course, there may be different explanations for different strandings, depending on the species, location, and a variety of other factors.

Stranded sperm whale,
Horta, Faial, Azores

What should you do if you find a stranded animal?

Without human intervention, when a live whale, dolphin, or porpoise becomes stranded it usually dies. Cetaceans are not adapted to life on land—they quickly overheat and, out of the relatively weightless medium of the sea, their light bones cannot support their bodies and they literally crush themselves to death. Rescuing a stranded animal is extremely difficult and normally requires great skill and patience. Well intentioned, but misdirected, efforts can cause considerable stress to the animal and may even result in its death. It can also be quite dangerous to attempt a rescue, since even small cetaceans have been known to injure human helpers when they thrash around. Perhaps not surprisingly, in some countries it is illegal to give unauthorized first aid to any stranded cetacean.

These very basic guidelines are designed merely to make a stranded animal as comfortable as possible until expert help arrives. The golden rule in every case is to call the local police immediately and to attempt a rescue yourself only if expert help is unavailable.

■ Try to keep the animal upper-side up, taking care not to trap either of the flippers under its body, and never pushing or pulling on the flippers, flukes, or head.

■ Keep the animal's skin moist and cool, with wet towels or water, but be careful not to cover the blowhole (or to let either water or sand enter the blowhole).

■ Erect a shelter to provide shade from the sun, but never apply suntan lotion to the animal's skin.

■ Keep onlookers and their dogs at a distance, make as little noise as possible, and do not touch the animal more than necessary.

■ Never, under any circumstances, attempt to destroy a stranded animal yourself.

Spinner dolphin which
died after stranding,
Sri Lanka

How do they sleep?

The way in which whales, dolphins, and porpoises sleep has
baffled and intrigued scientists for a very long time. Aristotle
seemed particularly excited, centuries ago, when he noted
that "there are even people who have heard a dolphin snore."

Over the years, of course, there have been some
interesting theories. One was that they haul themselves out
of the sea after dark and then spend the night curled up on
shore in the company of seals and sea lions; no one had
actually seen them doing it, but the idea probably seemed
quite logical at the time. Another theory was that they simply
dive down to the seabed, make themselves comfortable, and
lie there for the night.

In fact, the truth is even stranger than the fiction. Unlike
most other mammals, cetaceans never fall into a deep sleep,
and they do not seem to have regular sleeping patterns
linked to night and day. They do sleep, of course, though not
in the way we might expect.

The reason is simple. Since our breathing is automatic, we can safely sleep and breathe at the same time. But cetaceans control their breathing consciously, so they have to be awake, and able to think, in order to take regular breaths. If they were to fall into a deep sleep, which is a naturally occurring state of unconsciousness, they would then drown.

Keiko, a captive killer whale used in the *Free Willy* movies, in Oregon

Instead of long periods of deep sleep, their solution is to swim along slowly, or lie just below the surface, and take short "catnaps." They are believed to go into a semi-conscious state by switching off one half of the brain at a time. Then they swap sides to ensure that both halves are fully rested. While one side of the brain is asleep, the other remains awake to control the breathing and, of course, to look out for predators.

Should they be kept in captivity?
During the past century, more than 25 species of whales, dolphins, and porpoises have been kept in captivity in zoos, marine parks, and aquaria around the world. Thousands of individual animals have been captured in the wild, sometimes

for research or military purposes, but mainly to perform special shows for the fee-paying public. They are trained to jump through hoops, balance balls on their heads, "kiss" their trainers, perform somersaults and synchronized leaps, and to do many other tricks for the millions of people who flock to see them every year.

Their owners argue that the animals "enjoy" the shows, and are fortunate to be safe from predators, pollution, and other threats in the wild. They point out that, as the undisputed stars of zoos and marine parks, they are worth a great deal of money and, directly or indirectly, provide thousands of people with secure jobs. They also claim that captive animals encourage members of the public to take an interest in the conservation of their wild relatives.

Some facilities are obviously much better than others, and whales and dolphins are kept in a bewildering range of establishments, from dirty hotel pools to professional marine parks with large, coastal enclosures that are filled naturally with seawater and flushed with every new tide. Many of the animals are treated abominably, while a very lucky few receive the best possible care and attention.

But most conservation and animal welfare groups are strongly opposed to keeping whales, dolphins, or porpoises in captivity of any kind. They say that it is immoral and cruel. Taken from the wild, and separated from their well structured family groups, the animals are often forced to live alone or with unfamiliar species. Many of them are kept in small and featureless concrete tanks, where they can no longer hunt or hear the sounds of the sea, and may even be deprived of natural sunlight. At the same time, they have to eat dead fish and cope with hordes of noisy people watching them day after day.

To make matters worse, few zoos or marine parks make a genuine effort to educate the public, or "educate" them with inaccurate information, so the real benefits and spin-offs for their wild relatives are very limited. In conclusion it would seem there is little doubt that most captive animals are there simply to provide cheap entertainment for profit.

Will we ever be able to talk to them?

Whales, dolphins, and porpoises are known to communicate in two main ways: by sound and with body language. They may even be telepathic, as well, and thus able to communicate without speech or movement.

But current evidence suggests that they probably do not have a true language. While they can pass on information such as danger, irritation, or sexual interest, they probably cannot complain about the poor size of fish, discuss the vagaries of the weather, or talk about their plans for the future. In other words, they can give simple commands and signals, but probably cannot discuss more abstract concepts.

However, there is no doubt that we still have a great deal to learn about their communication skills. Some dolphins, for example, seem to have their own "signature whistles," which are almost the equivalent of human names. They use these to attract the attention of other dolphins and to identify themselves; there is even some evidence to suggest that one dolphin will call the name of another in its group.

In captivity, research also demonstrates that they can grasp the essential elements of any human language. They do not actually speak, of course, but they can respond correctly to sentences up to five words long. This suggests that they have the *potential* to develop a language, even if they have not done so in the wild.

Humpback whale with whale watchers, eastern USA

Whether or not we will ever be able to communicate with them is another matter altogether. In the past, people predicted that we would be conversing with dolphins, and other small cetaceans, within a few decades; others went so far as to suggest that if an alien intelligence were to attempt to communicate with life on Earth, it might choose dolphins in preference to humans. But these are dreams that have yet to come true.

How do they find their way around?

Whales, dolphins, and porpoises find their way around their underwater world in ways that are well beyond the scope of our own senses. Most of them retain the senses of sight, touch, and taste, but they rely mainly on hearing. They are also believed to have an extra sense, known as geomagnetism, which enables them to detect the Earth's magnetic field.

Killer whale, northern Norway

The ability to see varies greatly from one species to another. While some of the river dolphins are virtually blind, for example, most marine cetaceans can see fairly well in both air and water. However, sight is of limited benefit to them since they spend so much of their lives in the dark depths or in turbid water where visibility is poor even close to the surface.

Hearing is far more important. Effective at night as well as during the day, it does not rely on good visibility. At the same time, sound travels through water nearly five times faster than through air and can be heard over much longer distances. Although cetaceans have lost the distinctive outer ear flaps typical of most other mammals, they do have ears in the form of tiny holes in the skin behind their eyes. Many species can probably also receive sounds through their lower jaws.

The senses of taste and smell are very similar, because they are both used to detect chemicals. It is possible to smell underwater: sharks, for example, can smell chemicals in the water from a long distance away. But toothed whales have probably lost their sense of smell altogether, and baleen whales retain only a rudimentary form—mainly because their nostrils (or blowholes) have to remain tightly shut when they dive. Taste is far more important and is used for detecting chemicals both inside and near the outside of the mouth.

Whales, dolphins, and porpoises also have very sensitive skin and are able to use their dorsal fins, flippers, and beaks to investigate unfamiliar objects, and to touch one another as a form of greeting, or to strengthen social bonds.

Geomagnetism is undoubtedly the least known of all the senses. It involves detecting or "reading" the Earth's magnetic field, possibly using it like an invisible "map" to navigate over large distances. Many animals, from bacteria and bees to reptiles and birds, are believed to have this sixth sense. It may even exist to a limited degree in humans— what we identify in ourselves simply as a "sense of direction." But it seems to be particularly well developed in many cetaceans, and may help them to navigate their way across the world's seas and oceans.

Whales and dolphins are believed to "read" the Earth's magnetic field like an invisible "map"

What is echolocation?

Most whales, dolphins, and porpoises have a remarkable sensory system, called echolocation, which enables them to build up a "picture" of their underwater surroundings with the help of sound. Bats, shrews, cave swiftlets, oilbirds, and a number of other land-based animals use a similar system to hunt fast-moving prey in the dark.

The basic principle of the echolocation system used by cetaceans is quite simple. They transmit ultrasonic clicks into the water, and then monitor and interpret any echoes that bounce back. The clicks are believed to be produced within the nasal plugs, or in the larynx, and are then focused into a directional beam by the fatty "melon" (which appears as a rounded forehead on most species). The returning echoes may be picked up by the small ear holes on either side of the head. Recent research suggests that they are more likely to be transmitted to the brain via the lower jaw.

Common dolphin, Mexico

Echolocation is actually a form of sonar (radar works in a similar way, but uses electromagnetic radiation instead of sound). However, the system used by many cetaceans is so complex and sophisticated that it leaves human sonar experts gasping. The human system, though useful, is little more than a crude imitation by comparison. When homing in on a fish, for example, a dolphin can use echolocation to identify the fish's size and shape, which way it is swimming, its texture, and possibly even its internal structure.

Toothed whales are the real echolocation experts. They use it for keeping track of one another, navigating around objects in the water, identifying changes in sea-floor profile, hunting, and monitoring the surroundings for potential predators or prey. It is even possible that some toothed whales may be able to use particularly powerful blasts of ultrasonic clicks to stun or kill their prey. Baleen whales may also be able to echolocate, but this has never been proven and any sonar system they do have is probably much less well developed. How baleen whales find their food is still largely a mystery.

Echolocation at work

Record breakers

Largest: The blue whale is the largest animal on Earth. The average adult length is 82 feet in males and 86 feet in females, with body weights of 90–120 tons. The heaviest ever recorded was a female, caught in the Southern Ocean on March 20, 1947, which weighed 190 tons. The longest ever recorded was another female, landed in 1909 at Grytviken, South Georgia, in the South Atlantic, which measured 110 feet from the tip of her snout to the end of her tail.

Blue whale, Sea of Cortez, Mexico

Smallest: It is very difficult to identify the world's smallest cetacean, partly because there is so much variation between individuals. Taking the maximum known length as a guide, it is a competition between Hector's dolphin (4 feet 6 inches for the smaller male) and the vaquita (4 feet 9 inches also for the smaller male).

Longest flippers: The longest flippers belong to the humpback whale. They grow to 23–31 percent of the length of the whale—making a potential maximum of more than 18 feet—but typically measure around 15 feet in fully grown animals. They are used to herd fish, to maneuver while swimming, to comfort their young, and to slap the surface of the water.

Humpback whale, New England

Tallest dorsal fin: The huge, triangular dorsal fin of the bull killer whale can reach a remarkable height of 6 feet, which makes it roughly as tall as a man. In comparison, the blue whale's dorsal fin is relatively small, rarely reaching more than 16 inches in height.

Longest baleen plate: The longest baleen is found in the bowhead whale. There are many records within the 10- to 13-foot range, but lengths of up to 17 feet have been reported for animals killed during the nineteenth century.

Longest tooth: The male narwhal has two teeth. The one on the right normally remains invisible, but the one on the left grows to a remarkable length. It pierces the animal's upper lip, develops into a long tusk and eventually looks rather like a gnarled and twisted walking stick. At least one-third of all narwhal tusks are broken, but unbroken tusks reach an average length of just over six feet. In extreme cases, they have been known to exceed 10 feet and weigh more than 22 pounds.

Bowhead whale, Nunavut, Arctic Canada

Thickest blubber: The blubber of the bowhead whale is thicker than in any other animal, averaging an incredible 17–20 inches. It provides the whale with protection against the freezing cold waters of its Arctic home.

Tallest blow: The "blow" or "spout" is the cloud of condensed air and water droplets produced above a whale's head when it blows out. The tallest blow is made by the blue whale: slender and vertical in shape, it can reach an astonishing height of 50 feet, which is clearly visible from several miles away.

Fastest: On 12 October 1958, a bull killer whale was timed swimming at 34.5 mph in the eastern North Pacific. Similar speeds, albeit in short bursts, have also been reported for Dall's porpoises.

Largest appetite: The largest blue whales probably eat as much as 5.5 tons of krill (*see* page 17), every day. Even an average-sized blue whale is believed to eat about four tons. Since each of these tiny animals weighs only around .035 ounces, a daily intake of about four million of them is required to keep the whale going. In terms of weight, this is equivalent to eating a fully grown African elephant every day. The whale does not feed all year round, but gorges itself all summer and then fasts during the winter.

Largest prey: Killer whales have been known to prey on more than 25 different whale and dolphin species—and there have been several reported attacks on sperm whales and blues. The largest giant squid known to be taken by a sperm whale was 47 feet 6 inches long, including its tentacles; it was caught on Great Bahama Bank, Bahamas.

Noisiest: The low-frequency booms made by blue whales and fin whales when vocalizing across enormous stretches of ocean have been measured at up to 188 decibels, making them the loudest sounds emitted by any living source. These remarkable sounds are below the range of human hearing, but with the right equipment they can be detected over distances of up to 1,865 miles. It is not yet clear whether they are used for long-distance communication or are part of a long-range sonar navigation system for detecting underwater features such as seamounts.

Longest-lived: It is difficult to measure the age of a whale accurately, so the maximum lifespan is not known for most species. However, indirect evidence suggests that some of the larger whales, at least, are able to reach a grand old age of considerably more than 100 years. In 1995, a freshly-killed bowhead whale was being processed in Alaska when the Inuit hunters found two stone harpoon blades embedded in its blubber. Since the use of these particular harpoons ended a century ago, the animal must have been at least 100 years old—and might have survived a lot longer if it had not been killed by people. Meanwhile, scientists have developed a way

Fin whale, New England

of determining the ages of some whales by examining the amino acids in the lenses of their eyes. Limited evidence from this research suggests that another bowhead whale in Alaska may have been 211 years old when killed.

Shortest-lived: The lifespan for many small cetaceans, in particular, is unknown and it is very difficult to be certain of the shortest. One possible contender is Burmeister's porpoise, which has not been known to live beyond 12 years. But this is a poorly known species and future research may increase this figure.

Longest migration: Humpback whales are inveterate travelers and their migrations are phenomenal—the longest known of any mammal. In 1990, for example, one particular humpback was identified by American biologists off the Antarctic Peninsula; less then five months later, it was

Sperm whales, Sea of Cortez, Mexico

identified by Colombian biologists off their own coast, north of the equator. It had traveled almost 5,405 miles. Since then, several other humpbacks have been identified in both Antarctica and Colombia, confirming that the first individual was not simply lost.

Deepest diver: Sperm whales can dive for longer than two hours to depths of at least 6,560 feet and probably deeper.

Most acrobatic: Many whales, dolphins, and porpoises are known for their aerial displays. Among the larger species, right whales, humpback whales, and killer whales are particularly acrobatic. Humpbacks have been known to leap almost clear of the water more than 80 times in a row, which is a phenomenal achievement considering an average-sized humpback weighs the equivalent of 400 people. There are also many outstanding acrobats in the dolphin family. Bottlenose, spotted, striped, dusky, and other dolphins have been known to hurl themselves as high as 23 feet into the air and frequently turn somersaults before reentering the water. But perhaps the most spectacular acrobat is the spinner dolphin, which leaps high into the air, then spins around on its longitudinal axis as many as seven times before splashing back into the water.

Most contaminated: Belugas living in the Gulf of St. Lawrence, Canada, are so badly contaminated with heavy metals, organochlorines, and benzoapyrene that, when they die, their bodies could qualify as toxic waste.

Most studied: A number of individual whales and dolphins have been studied in the wild for many years. One of the most studied is a female humpback whale called Salt. She was first sighted on May 1, 1976 by biologists studying the whales around Stellwagen Bank, off the coast of New England. She has been observed and photographed by dozens of scientists, and thousands of whale-watchers, around Stellwagen Bank and nearby Jeffery's Ledge every summer since. Salt has also been studied in her Caribbean breeding grounds for many years, since she was first sighted off the coast of the Dominican Republic in 1978.

CONSERVATION

Endangered species

To the best of our knowledge, no whale, dolphin, or porpoise has become extinct in modern times (although no one is certain about the status of the Baiji). But a frightening number are in serious trouble, and others have all but disappeared from many of their former haunts.

Considering the magnitude of the problems they face, the odds are firmly stacked against them and, for some at least, the future is undoubtedly bleak.

It is difficult to judge which species is the most endangered. Unfortunately, our knowledge is so inadequate that there are no widely accepted population estimates for the vast majority. Several beaked whales, for example, are known only from stranded specimens and have never been seen alive—but the total lack of observations in the wild does not necessarily mean they are rare, especially since few beaked whales are seen

Some of the rarest whales, dolphins, and porpoises in the world

	SPECIES	DISTRIBUTION
1	Baiji	Yangtze river, China (middle and lower reaches)
2	North Atlantic and North Pacific right whales	North Atlantic and North Pacific
3	Vaquita or Gulf of California porpoise	Extreme northern end of the Gulf of California (Sea of Cortez), Mexico
4	Indus river dolphin	Main channel of the Indus River, Pakistan, downstream of Chashma Barrage
5	Hector's dolphin	Coastal waters of New Zealand (most common around South Island)

regularly. At the same time, the number of survivors is not the only consideration. The blue whale, for example, is not one of the rarest cetaceans in the world but, after decades of intensive whaling, its chances of recovery are severely limited because it is a particularly slow breeder and because its obliterated population is widely dispersed.

The table below summarizes five of the rarest whales, dolphins, and porpoises for which population figures are known. Of course, it is possible that some poorly known species are even rarer than the ones on this list.

Baiji, Wuhan, China

Population	Notes
Likely to be in the low tens or extinct	Now very little chance of rescuing this species, which is likely to become the first cetacean known to become extinct
300 in the North Atlantic; a few hundred in the North Pacific	Hunted almost to extinction by commercial whalers and has never recovered
Fewer than 600	Has the most restricted distribution of any marine cetacean; most commonly seen around the Colorado River delta
Fewer than 1,000	The many threats to its survival include pollution, hunting, fishing, and the construction of dams
Fewer than 3,000	Threatened mainly by entanglement in coastal gillnets (may have reduced population by 50 percent since 1970)

Whaling

Coastal communities around the world have killed whales for centuries. The blubber and meat provides a welcome source of light, heat, and food that is sometimes essential for human survival.

In the old days, this small-scale subsistence hunting probably had only a local impact on whale populations, but by the end of the seventeenth century the character of whaling had changed beyond all recognition. In an age before petroleum or plastics, whales provided valuable raw materials for thousands of everyday products, from soap and candles to whips and corsets. There were huge profits to be made and whaling rapidly became big business.

The slaughter reached its worst excesses around the middle of the last century, thanks largely to a series of technological advances in whaling vessels, killing equipment, and processing methods. In 1930–31, for example, a record 30,000 blue whales were killed, and in 1963–64, no fewer than 29,255 sperm whales were killed.

Indigenous whaling in the Caribbean

One by one the great whales were hunted almost to the point of extinction. In the space of a few hundred years, literally millions of them were killed around the world. Today, we are left merely with the tattered remains: in most cases, no more than five to 10 percent of their original populations. There are barely 300 surviving North Atlantic right whales, the bowhead has all but disappeared from vast areas of its former range, and so the catalog of destruction unfolds. During the twentieth century, more than two million whales were killed in the southern hemisphere alone.

Yet, incredibly, we still have not learned the lessons of the past. The story of commercial whaling continues as Norway, Iceland, and Japan persist in hunting whales in the North Atlantic, the North Pacific and the Antarctic. In blatant defiance of world opinion, they are gradually expanding their activities and, alarmingly, they are being watched with considerable interest by other nations that may ultimately decide to resume whaling themselves.

To make matters even worse, it is virtually impossible to kill whales humanely. In some cases, it can take as long as an hour for them to die agonizing deaths after explosive harpoons have blown huge, gaping holes in their bodies. As one former whaler commented: "If whales could scream, whaling would have stopped many years ago."

Commercial whaling in Iceland

The hunt for the Faroese pilot whale

Large whales are not the only cetaceans to suffer from hunting. It is believed that tens of thousands of small whales, dolphins, and porpoises are killed every year in seas and oceans around the world, although the true extent of the problem is unknown. Nets, knives, rifles, hand-held, and even explosive, harpoons are used for the killing.

One of the most controversial of these hunts takes place in the Faroes, a group of islands lying halfway between Scotland and Iceland in the northeast Atlantic. Entire pods of long-finned pilot whales (as well as several dolphin species caught up in the hunt incidentally) are herded into sandy bays by men in small boats, during noisy "drives" that frequently take many hours to complete. All the animals—including pregnant and lactating females and their babies—are dragged ashore with steel hooks, called gaffs, and then killed with long knives.

Faroese hunting statistics date back to 1584, with unbroken records from 1709 to the present day. During this most recent 295-year period, more than one-quarter of a million long-finned pilot whales have been killed in approximately 1,700 different drives. The official number of whales taken each year ranges from zero to a peak of 4,385 recorded in 1941. An average of around 1,200 whales have been taken each year during the past decade.

The Faroese defend the hunt vigorously, arguing that it is a traditional part of their culture and provides a free and welcome source of protein. But opponents of the hunt argue that it is terribly cruel and no longer necessary in such a modern society with a relatively high standard of living; they also argue that no one knows enough about the number of pilot whales around the Faroes, their wider distribution and movements throughout the year, or any of the other dangers they face, to judge whether or not the hunt is a threat to their future survival.

Ironically, recent evidence suggests that it may actually be dangerous to eat long-finned pilot whales taken from the North Atlantic. Their meat and blubber have been found to contain high levels of toxic chemicals and could seriously threaten the health of the Faroese people. At the same time, of course, the presence of so many pollutants inevitably raises concern about the fitness of the whales themselves.

Whale meat drying in the Faroe Islands

Conflicts with fisheries

Since the 1950s, the staggering growth of many modern fisheries and the introduction of increasingly destructive fishing methods have spelled disaster for whales, dolphins, and porpoises around the world.

Hundreds of thousands of them—possibly millions—die slow, lingering deaths in fishing nets every year. Many more could be threatened by the sheer scale of modern fisheries, which overexploit fish stocks with scant regard for the future health of the world's oceans. And in some parts of the world fishermen intentionally kill cetaceans and other marine mammals, either to use as bait or because they view them as competition for "their" fish. Not surprisingly, few scientists are in any doubt that fishing is the single greatest human-induced cause of mortality in cetaceans.

Drift-netting is one of the worst culprits and, indeed, is probably the most indiscriminate method of fishing ever devised. Hanging in the water, unseen and undetectable, drift nets are carried freely with the ocean currents and winds. Dubbed "walls of death," or "curtains of death," they can be hundreds of miles long and catch everything in their path from seabirds and turtles to whales and dolphins. In the late 1980s, for instance, the Japanese high-seas squid drift-net fisheries in the North Pacific were killing approximately 15,000–30,000 northern rightwhale dolphins, 11,000 Pacific white-sided dolphins, and 6,000 Dall's porpoises every year. The United Nations took action by calling on all member nations to agree to a moratorium on drift-netting by the end of 1992. The global ban has had a very positive impact, but it is being ignored by some Asian countries and whales, dolphins, and porpoises continue to be killed in large numbers by drift nets deployed inside the 200-nautical-mile limit of many coastal states. More recently, the European Union banned drift-netting in almost all its waters, so progress is being made—albeit too slowly.

Gill nets are similar to drift nets in design, although much smaller, and pose another serious threat. Since they are relatively inexpensive, these deathtraps are used along coastlines and in major rivers worldwide, from New Zealand and Sri Lanka to Canada and Britain. Tens of thousands of small cetaceans are believed to drown in them every year.

But perhaps the most infamous culprit, responsible for killing more dolphins in the past 35 years than any other human activity, is the tuna-fishing industry. In the eastern tropical Pacific, a stretch of ocean extending from southern California to Chile and covering an area roughly the size of Canada, it has directly caused the deaths of an estimated six to 12 million dolphins. In the worst period, during the 1960s and early 1970s, as many as half a million dolphins were being killed in the region every year. The eastern spinner dolphin stock was reduced to 44 percent of its original size in just a few years. Fortunately, public outrage has forced the authorities to introduce new rules and regulations, which include releasing dolphins from the nets when they are captured, and the scale of the slaughter has dropped to thousands (rather than hundreds of thousands) of deaths a year. It is still too many, though, and the effects of stress from capture are an ongoing concern. There is also mounting evidence to suggest that dolphins are being set on by tuna-fishing fleets in other parts of the world.

Unfortunately, there are no easy solutions to most conflicts with fisheries. In some cases, a simple modification of the nets or the fishery management systems can have a positive effect. Educational programs for fishermen, and newly developed devices that alert whales and dolphins to the presence of nets, may also work in some situations. But there is no escaping the fact that much more drastic action, such as seasonal closures of some fisheries or dramatic changes in fishing techniques, may be the only effective long-term solution.

Fish on the floor of a fish market, Male, Maldives

Pollution

Some experts predict that pollution could become the most serious threat to whales, dolphins, and porpoises in the future. It is a silent, insidious, and widespread killer that is already causing severe problems around the world.

Despite all the warnings, many governments continue to pretend that the world's seas and oceans have an infinite capacity to absorb the waste products of human activities. Ever-increasing quantities of industrial waste, agricultural chemicals, radioactive discharges, untreated sewage, oil, modern plastic debris, and a wide variety of other pollutants are dumped directly into the sea every day—or slowly make their way there via rivers—often with devastating effect.

We are only just beginning to learn about the precise details of the damage they cause. Some pollutants are so toxic, or present in such huge quantities, that they cause immediate death. Others are more subtle in their effects, but nonetheless may be responsible for weeks, months, or even years of prolonged suffering. They gradually weaken the

Rubbish on beach in Baja California, Mexico

animals, causing hormonal imbalances, a lowering of disease resistance, cancer, and many other abnormalities and chronic health problems; they may even cause a loss of fertility.

Unfortunately, whales, dolphins, porpoises, and other top predators are particularly vulnerable to pollution. This is because the toxins are passed along the food chain. Minute quantities are picked up by marine plankton, which are then eaten by fish and squid, and these in turn are eaten by the predators themselves. The further along the chain, the higher the concentration of toxins. Worse still, much of this buildup is passed on from one generation to another: a lactating female, through her milk, can deliver the toxins in highly concentrated doses to her young calf.

Habitat degradation, disturbance, and noise pollution

One of the greatest threats to wildlife on land is habitat degradation, whether it be tropical rainforest destruction, desertification, wetland drainage, or road building across important grasslands and heathland. Whales, dolphins, and porpoises also suffer from habitat degradation and disturbance, although in different ways.

The main problem areas are rivers, areas close to the shore, and places near human activities farther out to sea. Coastal and riverbank development, land reclamation, deep-sea dumping, oil, gas and mineral exploration, commercial fish farming, boat traffic, and the effects of land-based activities such as deforestation and river damming are all to blame. Their consequences can be quite subtle, such as increased amounts of sediment or changes in salinity, but they can also be extremely dramatic. Habitat degradation along the coast, for example, can have a far-reaching impact on the marine environment as a whole, since this is where nurseries for all kinds of invertebrates and fish form the foundation of the sea's complex food webs.

River dolphins are probably hit hardest by habitat degradation. The threats their habitats face include heavy boat traffic, riverbank development, and dam construction.

In the case of the highly endangered Baiji, for example, the world's largest hydroelectric project at the famous Three Gorges, in Hubei Province, China is likely to be the final nail in its coffin.

To make matters worse, many of the species and populations most affected by habitat degradation already have restricted distributions, or their requirements tie them to coasts or rivers and prevent them from "escaping" to safer areas. These include all the river dolphins, the vaquita, Burmeister's porpoise, Hector's dolphin, and several large whales that move inshore at certain times of the year to breed.

Even whale watching can be a threat, if it is unregulated. Short-finned pilot whales living off the coast of Tenerife, in the Canary Islands, for example, face a veritable onslaught of whale-watch boats almost every day of the year. Many of the skippers are untrained and unconcerned about their impact on the whales, and their cavalier attitude could affect the long-term survival of the population.

One solution to the problem of habitat degradation and disturbance is to provide the animals with special sanctuaries, or marine reserves, in which they can feed and breed in relative safety. Some already exist, such as around Antarctica and in the Indian Ocean, but they need better legislation to be truly effective. And, of course, many more are needed.

But even marine sanctuaries cannot protect cetaceans from underwater noise pollution. Caused by a variety of human activities, from coastal development and seismic testing to speed boats and heavy shipping, this is a particular problem for whales, dolphins, and porpoises because they rely on sound for many of their day-to-day activities. Unfortunately, it is not only the loudness of a noise that is important, but its frequency as well—some frequencies are likely to be more disturbing than others, depending on the hearing range of different species. Noise may displace the animals from their feeding or breeding areas and can disrupt critical behaviors such as feeding or caring for young calves. Extremely loud noise can even kill them.

The U.S. Navy's LFAS (Low Frequency Active Sonar) has been in the news a great deal recently—and deservedly so.

Other nations are already operating or planning to operate similar systems within the next few years. LFAS relies on extremely loud, low-frequency sound to detect submarines at great distances and, according to the US Navy's own studies, generates sounds of up to 140 decibels more than 310 miles away from the sonar source. During testing off the California coast, the noise was detected on the other side of the North Pacific.

There is growing evidence that this system is extremely harmful to cetaceans—with several mass strandings in different parts of the world coinciding with the testing of military sonar. In September 2002, for example, a mass stranding of three species of beaked whales (totaling 15 animals) occurred during European naval excercises off the Canary Islands. Research has identified a condition in at least some of the animals that resembles decompression sickness (the "bends"), which occurs in divers who surface too quickly. It is possible that exposure to loud noise caused the whales to ascend faster than their physiology is adapted to allow. The only good news is that, following a legal ruling in 2003, peacetime use of LFAS by the U.S. military has now been significantly limited.

Copacabana Beach, Brazil

HOW TO WATCH WHALES, DOLPHINS, AND PORPOISES

Watching whales responsibly

It is sometimes easy to forget that we are uninvited guests in the world of whales, dolphins, and porpoises. We are privileged to see them, but do not have a divine right. In fact, we have a responsibility to cause as little disturbance as possible, which is why whale watching should be an eyes-on, hands-off activity.

Fortunately, most whale-watching operators care about the whales, and their guests, and do a good job. They abide by local regulations or codes of conduct and put the welfare of the animals before everything else, being careful not to disturb or injure them by maneuvering their boats carefully, slowly, and not too close, and then leaving before the whales

Friendly gray whale, San Ignacio Lagoon, Mexico

show signs of distress. A few operators, however, are not so careful and cause a great deal of unnecessary stress. Not only are the animals forced to steer clear of boats, or possibly even to abandon their preferred feeding or breeding grounds altogether, but collisions and other accidents can cause serious injury and even death.

The best trips also have knowledgable naturalists on board to keep everyone well informed; they provide free places for biologists to do urgently needed research, and they help raise money for whale conservation. They even play a valuable role in the local economy because, with a little planning and coordination, museums, science centers, bookshops, gift shops, bus companies, hotels and guesthouses, restaurants and cafés, taxi companies, and many other businesses can all benefit from the tremendous influx of visitors coming to see the whales.

In this way, the best operators put something back for the whales. Educational trips help drum up public support for their cause; the biologists learn more about their lives and needs; there is more money available to tackle important conservation issues; and the local people have good reason to look after the whales and their marine environment.

But ultimately, of course, it is the responsibility of individual whale watchers to choose the best and most responsible operators before booking a trip.

Clothing and equipment

The ideal choice of clothing and equipment obviously depends on where, when, and how you intend to watch whales. But here are a few suggestions:

Suntan lotion and sun hat are essential to avoid sunburn and sunstroke, especially around midday. Because you are more likely to burn at sea than you are on land, use a high factor lotion.

Seasickness tablets or patches should be taken or applied in plenty of time before the trip, if you have any doubts about suffering from seasickness.

Polaroid sunglasses help to reduce the sun's glare and are excellent for seeing through reflections on the surface of the water. Remember to attach them to a safety cord.

Waterproof bags are essential for protecting your spare clothing, binoculars, cameras, and other equipment from salty air and spray.

Waterproof jacket and trousers are important if sea conditions are likely to be rough or if you are expecting rain. Spending a day, or even half a day, soaked through to the skin can ruin an entire trip.

Warm and windproof clothing is vital if you are whale

watching in cold weather. Remember that it is much colder at sea than it is on shore. Be careful not to underestimate how many layers you are likely to need.

Rubber-soled deck shoes are important in case the deck gets wet with spray. It is easy to slip if you are wearing inappropriate shoes.

Field notebook and pen are invaluable (some people prefer a pocket-sized dictaphone instead). It's a good idea to copy your notes into a neat version later.

Identification guides are useful for identifying the whales, dolphins, or porpoises you encounter. Consider taking guides to the birds, seals, fish, and other local wildlife as well.

Binoculars are invaluable for finding whales, dolphins, and porpoises, as well as for identifying them and studying their behavior. Choose image-stabilized binoculars, or a normal pair with a magnification of 7–10x (anything higher will be unusable while you are bouncing around on a boat at sea).

Watching southern right whales, Western Cape, South Africa

A telescope (with tripod) can be useful when watching whales from shore, or from the relatively stable platform of a large cruise ship, but the high magnification makes it virtually unusable on smaller boats.

A camera with an 80–200mm lens (or a similar zoom) is ideal but, alternatively, a fixed lens of at least 135mm can be useful for recording close encounters and interesting behavior patterns. A motordrive is also useful. Do not forget to take plenty of film (at least twice as much as you think you will need) or, if you are using digital, plenty of card space. Use a medium to fast speed (100–200 ISO) depending on the weather and sea conditions.

Hydrophone (underwater microphone). Few whale watchers carry hydrophones because they are very expensive and can be difficult to use. But they do help you find some whales by sound, as well as adding a new and exciting dimension to the whale-watching experience.

Safety equipment should be provided on all organized whale-watching trips. This might include life jackets, life rafts, flares, a VHF radio, and first-aid equipment.

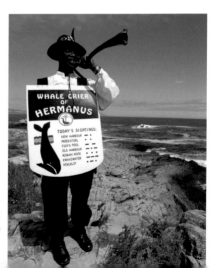

Whale crier,
South Africa

Finding the animals at sea

In theory, it is possible to see whales, dolphins, and porpoises almost anywhere in the world. They are found near the poles, at the equator, in freshwater rivers, along shallow coastlines, and even in the deep waters of the open sea.

But many species tend to be plentiful only in particular areas and, even then, are present only at certain times of the year. Their distribution also varies weekly, daily, and hourly, according to many different factors such as sea and weather conditions, food availability, and human disturbance. To add to the challenge, they can be very difficult to spot in anything but the calmest conditions—even if you are very close to them.

People with a lot of experience at sea instinctively recognize the tiniest clues when they are looking for cetaceans. They are trained to register the slightest movements and splashes that give their presence away. With a large whale, for example, the first clue is often its blow or spout. This is more visible in some weather conditions than others, but it can be surprisingly distinctive. It may look like a flash of white (especially against a dark background) or a more gradual puff of smoke. Blows are easy to miss, though, especially since there is often a considerable gap between each one.

Challenging conditions on the Drake Passage

Alternatively, you may briefly see the head and back of the whale break the surface. This often resembles a strange wave that, somehow, does not look quite right. Anything suspicious, even if nine times out of 10 it does turn out to be a wave, is worth investigating. Splashes are also good clues. They can be caused by a large whale breaching, flipper-slapping, or lobtailing—or by dolphins. A group of dolphins in the distance frequently looks like a rough patch of water, resembling lots of whitecaps and little breaking waves. The presence of birds can often be a telltale sign as well, particularly if they seem to be feeding or are concentrated in one particular area. It makes sense that, if they have found a school of fish, there could be whales or dolphins feeding underneath.

Finally, do not forget to look *everywhere*—in front, behind, and to both sides. Scan the horizon with binoculars and use the naked eye to check nearer the boat (it is amazing how often people miss dolphins bow-riding right in front of them because they are too busy looking far out to sea). The golden rule is to be patient because, even in areas with well known cetacean populations, it may take a while to track them down.

Problems of identification

Identifying whales, dolphins, and porpoises at sea is a real challenge. In fact, it can be so difficult that even the world's experts are unable to identify every species they encounter. On most official surveys, at least some sightings have to be logged as "unidentified." But despite the inevitable frustrations, developing the necessary skills to tell one species from another can also be very satisfying.

There are a number of different problems to overcome. The first, quite simply, is being on a boat. Making detailed observations while trying to keep your balance on a rolling, slippery deck can be difficult at the best of times. Adverse sea and weather conditions, such as a heavy swell, whitecaps, high winds, driving rain, or even glaring sunshine, add to the difficulties by making it almost impossible to get a good view and an accurate impression of the main features of the animal.

Then there are the whales, dolphins, and porpoises themselves. They spend most of their lives underwater and, even when they come to the surface to breathe, frequently reveal little more than a brief glimpse of their dorsal fins and backs. Even a good view can be confusing, since many species look alike: it takes a highly trained eye to tell the difference between a pygmy sperm whale and a dwarf sperm whale, for example.

At the same time, individuals of the same species frequently vary so much that they are rarely identical. Their dorsal fins are shaped differently, they show variations in their coloring, behave differently, and even come in a range of different sizes. Adult bottlenose dolphins, for example, vary in size from just under seven feet to nearly 13 feet.

However, despite all these potential pitfalls, it is still possible for anyone to recognize the relatively common and distinctive species and, eventually, many of the more unusual ones as well. It just requires some background knowledge and a little practice.

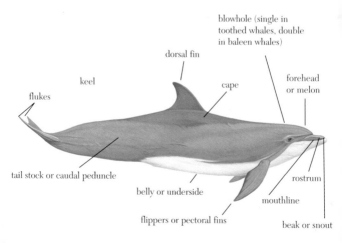

blowhole (single in toothed whales, double in baleen whales)

dorsal fin

keel

cape

forehead or melon

flukes

tail stock or caudal peduncle

belly or underside

flippers or pectoral fins

rostrum

mouthline

beak or snout

Identification checklist

The easiest way to identify whales, dolphins, and porpoises is to use a relatively simple process of elimination. This involves running through a mental checklist of 14 key features every time a new animal is encountered at sea. It is not often possible to use all 14 features, and one alone is rarely enough for a positive identification, but the best approach is to gather information on as many as possible before drawing any firm conclusions.

Geographical location: There is not a single place in the world where all 84 cetacean species have been recorded. In fact, there are not many places with records of more than a few dozen species. This immediately helps cut down on the number of possibilities. Atlantic white-sided dolphins, for example, occur only in the North Atlantic, while Pacific white-sided dolphins occur only in the North Pacific.

Habitat: Just as cheetahs live on open plains rather than in jungles, and snow leopards prefer mountains to wetlands, most whales, dolphins, and porpoises are adapted to specific marine or freshwater habitats. For example, Hector's dolphins are unlikely to be encountered far out to sea, while sperm whales are unlikely to be seen in shallow water.

Killer whale, northern Norway

Size: It is difficult to estimate size accurately at sea, unless a direct comparison can be made with the length of the boat or another object in the water. Therefore it is better to use three simple categories: up to 10 feet, 10 to 30 feet and more than 30 feet. In this way, simply by deciding whether the animal is small, medium, or large helps to eliminate a wide range of possibilities.

Unusual features: Some cetaceans have very unusual features that can be used for a quick identification. These include the extraordinary long tusk of the male narwhal and the callosities covering the heads of right whales.

Dorsal fin: The size, shape, and position of the dorsal fin varies greatly between species. Some fins are tall and triangular, others are rounded, a few are little more than a hump, some have broad bases, others have narrow bases, some are curved, others are upright, and there is every possible combination in between; and, of course, a few species have no dorsal fin at all. The position of the fin on the animal's back—in the middle, toward the head, or toward the tail—is also a useful identification feature.

Flippers: The length, color, and shape of the flippers, as well as their position on the animal's body, vary greatly from

Bryde's whale, Shikoku Island, Japan

Spinner dolphin, Maldives

one species to another. It is not always possible to see them, but flippers can be useful for identification in some species. In the humpback whale, for example, they are unmistakable.

Body shape: Much of the time, whales, dolphins, and porpoises do not show enough of themselves to provide an overall impression of their shape. Sometimes, however, this can be a useful feature. For example, the vaquita has a noticeably robust body shape, while the finless porpoise is quite slender and streamlined.

Beak: The presence or absence of a prominent beak is a particularly useful identification feature in toothed whales. The Irrawaddy dolphin, for instance, has a rounded head without an obvious beak, whereas the spinner dolphin has a very long, narrow beak.

Color and markings: Many cetaceans are surprisingly colorful, and have distinctive markings such as body stripes or eye patches. Commerson's dolphins, for example, are markedly black and white, while Risso's dolphins are usually covered in white scratches and scars. Unfortunately, more subtle markings can be difficult to use for identification purposes, because colors at sea vary according to water clarity and light conditions. Also, bear in mind that the animal can appear much darker than normal if it is viewed against the sun.

Flukes: The flukes can be important features for identifying larger whales. Some species lift their flukes high into the air before they dive, others do not. Minke and sei whales generally do not, for example, while humpbacks and sperm whales frequently do. It is also worth checking the shape of the flukes, looking for any distinctive markings and noticing whether or not there is a notch between the trailing edges.

Blow or spout: The blow is only really visible in larger whales. But it varies in height, shape, and visibility between species and, especially on calm days, can be extremely useful for identification purposes. Although variations in the blow between individuals can make it a tricky means of identification, experienced observers can tell one species from another even from a considerable distance. Right whales, for example, have wide, V-shaped blows, whereas fin whales produce single, narrow columns of spray.

Dive sequence: The dive sequence can be suprisingly distinctive in many species. Variations include: the angle at which the head breaks the surface; whether or not the dorsal fin and blowhole are visible at the same time; how strongly the tail stock is arched; the time interval between breaths; and the number of breaths before a deep dive.

Behavior: Some species are more active at the surface than others, so any unusual behavior can sometimes be useful for identification purposes. Among the large whales, for instance, humpbacks and right whales breach much more often than fin whales and blue whales.

Group size: Since some species are highly gregarious, while others tend to live alone or in small groups, it is worth making a note of the number of animals seen together. Fin whales, for example, are normally seen alone or in small groups, whereas there could be dozens or hundreds of long-finned pilot whales traveling together, or literally thousands of common dolphins.

Short-finned pilot whales, Sea of Cortez, Mexico

The golden rule

It is often tempting to guess the identification of an unusual whale, dolphin, or porpoise that you have not seen very clearly. But this is a mistake. Apart from the fact that it is bad science, it does little to improve your identification skills. Working hard at identification—and then enjoying the satisfaction of knowing that an animal has been identified correctly—is what makes you a real expert in the long term.

It is perfectly acceptable to record simply "unidentified dolphin" or "unidentified whale," if a more accurate identification is not possible. But do write detailed notes for reference at a later date. As well as helping improve your field skills, these notes may enable repeat sightings of species previously recorded as "unidentified" to be turned into a positive identification days, weeks, months, or even years later.

Recognizing behavior patterns

Whales, dolphins, and porpoises are active animals and some of their more impressive and energetic displays take place in full view on the surface of the water. They slap the water with their flippers, fins, or tails, ride in the bow waves and wakes of boats, lift their heads above the surface, and even leap high into the air and land back in the water with a tremendous splash.

Gray whale, San Ignacio Lagoon, Mexico

We do not fully understand the meaning of many of these displays and, of course, it is quite possible that there are different explanations for different occasions, according to the species, the age, and sex of the animal, and the context in which the activities are taking place.

However, a great deal of behavioral research has been done in recent years and, at last, we are beginning to unravel some of their secrets. Slapping the surface, for example, may be a form of courtship display, a way of signaling across great distances underwater, a technique for herding fish or dislodging parasites, a show of strength or a challenge...or, in some cases, it could simply be for fun.

Breaching: When a whale launches itself into the air head-first, and falls back into the water with a splash, it is said to be breaching. Most species have been observed breaching at one time or another, although some do it more often than others. Tail breaching is similar, but is tail-first instead of head-first and rarely lifts the whale as far out of the water.

Flipper-slapping: Many cetaceans lie on their sides or backs and slap one or both of their flippers onto the surface with a resounding splash. This is known as flipper-slapping, pectoral-slapping, pec-slapping, or flipper-flopping.

Lobtailing: Lobtailing is an impressive display, especially in large whales, involving the forceful slapping of the flukes against the surface of the water. Also known as tail-slapping, it is done while the main body of the whale lies just under the surface.

Southern right whale, Western Cape, South Africa

Blowing or spouting: The blow or spout is the cloud of condensed air and atomized water droplets (not water) produced above a whale's head when it breathes out. It is also the term used to describe the actual act of breathing. In most small whales, dolphins, and porpoises, the blow is low, brief, and barely visible, but in large whales it can be very distinctive.

Fluking: When some large whales make a deep dive from the surface, they lift their tails high into the air to thrust their bodies into a more steeply-angled descent toward deeper waters. Bowheads, right whales, grays, blues, humpbacks, and sperm whales all lift their flukes regularly, while a number of other species do from time to time. All whales leave a "flukeprint" at the surface—a circular swirl looking like a patch of oil—made by turbulence from the movement of the flukes.

Spyhopping: Spyhopping is the term used to describe an interesting form of behavior in which whales and dolphins poke their heads above the surface of the water, apparently to have a look around. Most species can see both above and below the surface.

Wake-riding: Swimming in the frothy wake of a boat or ship seems to be a favorite pastime of many dolphins, as well as some whales and porpoises. They surf, twist and turn in the waves, and even splash around and swim upside down in the bubbles.

Logging: It is not uncommon to see groups of whales floating motionless at the surface together, usually all facing in the same direction. Known as logging, this is a form of rest.

Porpoising: When traveling at speed, many cetaceans literally leave the water each time they take a breath. Also known as running, this is believed to reduce friction on their bodies when they break the surface, which may help conserve energy.

Bow-riding: Many dolphins, and some whales and porpoises, ride the bow-waves of boats and ships, jostling for the best position where they can be pushed along in the water by the force of the wave. Certain dolphins even ride the bow-waves of large whales in exactly the same way. On some occasions they may simply be hitching a free ride but, when they actively go out of their way to ride in the bow-waves, it is difficult to imagine that it can be anything more than exuberant play.

Bow-riding Heaviside's dolphins, Western Cape, South Africa

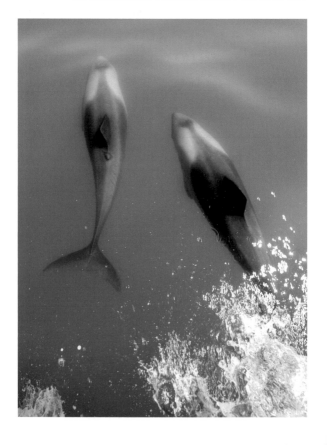

HOW WHALES AND DOLPHINS ARE STUDIED

Research on wild whales is staggeringly new. It is so new, in fact, that whale biologists have yet to monitor a single generation of large whales through one complete life cycle, from the moment they are born to their last days and ultimately to death through old age.

For years, the prospect of studying whales must have seemed about as difficult and challenging as exploring outer space. After all, these are animals that often live in extremely remote areas far out to sea, spend much of their lives diving to great depths underwater, and then show little of themselves when they rise to the surface to breathe. Many are quite shy and elusive, as well, and tend to avoid boats so, even at the surface, close encounters with them are almost impossible.

From early beginnings to high-tech research

For a long time, the only information we had came from dead animals washed ashore, or killed by fishermen, and from some of the millions of whales slaughtered by commercial whalers. Then scientists began to study captive bottlenose dolphins and other small cetaceans in their concrete tanks.

But as we accumulated a wealth of data on basic whale biology, our knowledge of their lives under natural conditions, wild and free, was severely limited. In the days when modern technology had already taken us to the Moon and beyond, we were only just beginning to understand these extraordinary forms of intelligent life on our own planet. As one biologist commented, "the best we can say is that our knowledge of whales, dolphins, and porpoises has progressed from almost nothing to just a little bit."

The first attempts at researching wild whales concentrated simply on counting whales—dead ones, initially, because they were so much easier to count than live ones. It was not until the late 1960s and early 1970s that a few pioneer biologists began the painstaking process of counting live whales, and then trying to learn more about their feeding techniques, breeding habits, migrations, and other aspects of their daily lives.

Gradually, more and more people became involved in whale research, and their information-gathering techniques became increasingly sophisticated. In the past decade, the number of researchers, projects, and study locations has increased exponentially, while whale research itself has become a leading branch of natural science.

Modern whale researchers still study whales in the traditional sense, simply watching them through binoculars, for example, or leaning out of boats to scoop up their feces for examination. But, at the same time, they frequently enlist the help of state-of-the-art equipment and the kind of enterprising and visionary research techniques that would make NASA proud.

Satellites in space, deep-sea submersibles, radio transmitters, high-tech directional hydrophones, complex computer programs, fiber optics, deepwater video probes,

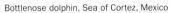

Bottlenose dolphin, Sea of Cortez, Mexico

DNA fingerprinting, and most recently, the U.S. Navy's Integrated Underwater Surveillance System are now all part of the modern whale researcher's armory.

Photo identification

Biologists have been identifying individual animals as part of their research for a long time. It is an invaluable way of following their movements, activities, and associations over periods of days, weeks, months, and even years. Jane Goodall used facial patterns to recognize all the chimpanzees in her classic study in Gombe National Park, Tanzania, for example; more recent studies have used striping patterns in zebras, the arrangement of whiskers in lions, and even the shapes, nicks, and scars of elephants' ears to tell one animal from another.

Whale and dolphin biologists are no exception, and they identify individuals in many different ways. Blue whales can be recognized by the shape of the dorsal fin and the pattern of mottling on the body; individual humpback whales, on the other hand, are recognized by the unique black-and-white markings on the underside of the tail. The differences can often be quite subtle, so each animal is photographed to confirm its identity and to provide a permanent record of its existence. This technique is known as "photo-identification," or "photo-ID," and has dramatically extended our knowledge of wild cetaceans in recent years.

DNA fingerprinting

Do different calves with the same mother share the same father? Are individuals that spend a lot of time together related? These and many other intriguing questions can be answered just by examining a small piece of a whale's skin. More accurately, it is the genetic material, or DNA, in the skin that is so revealing. Just as one person's fingerprints are different from everyone else's, no two animals have exactly the same DNA—yet related animals show some similarities. The clever detective work involved in interpreting this information is called "DNA fingerprinting," and it has proved invaluable in wild whale research.

Radio- and satellite-telemetry

It is possible to attach a specially-designed transmitter to a whale or dolphin and then follow its movements from a boat, a light aircraft, or even a research laboratory on the other side of the world. Some transmitters are merely tracking devices, but more sophisticated models can also provide information on the animal's swimming patterns, dive depths, and heart rate, as well as environmental conditions, water temperature, and much more. There are basically two kinds of transmitter: radio transmitters, which send signals directly to receivers nearby, and satellite transmitters, which beam the signals up to orbiting communications satellites and from there back to receiving stations anywhere on Earth.

Eavesdropping on the underwater world

Whales, dolphins, and porpoises live in a world that is dominated by sound, and a great deal can be learned by listening to them underwater. This is such a challenging area of research that it has been likened to trying to find out what goes on in New York City by dangling a microphone from the top of the Empire State Building. But experienced whale scientists using hydrophones (sophisticated underwater microphones), have been making some exciting discoveries in recent years.

A major development in this field came in 1992, when the U.S. Navy opened its doors to the so-called Integrated Underwater Surveillance System. A series of sophisticated underwater listening stations on the seabed, originally designed for tracking enemy submarines, this offers some tremendously exciting possibilities for whale research in the future.

The whale jigsaw

There are still no shortcuts in whale research but, in recent years, the growth in our knowledge has been nothing short of remarkable. Studying such elusive creatures is all about being content with tiny snippets of information that must be assembled into a coherent picture over periods of many years. It is like piecing together an enormously complicated jigsaw puzzle, where each piece brings with it new questions and unexpected surprises. The main difference, of course, is that the whale jigsaw will never be completely finished. Nevertheless, it is encouraging to know that we have probably added more pieces in the past 10 or 20 years than ever before.

Sperm whales,
Sea of Cortez,
Mexico

Gray Whale
Eschrichtius robustus

ID FACT FILE

OTHER NAMES
California gray
whale, mussel-
digger, devilfish,
scrag whale.

MAXIMUM LENGTH
49 feet.

MAXIMUM WEIGHT
35 tons.

FIELD ID
Mottled gray; low
hump instead of
fin; "knuckles"
between hump
and tail; low
heart-shaped
blow; narrow
head with
barnacles and
whale lice;
usually raises
flukes when
diving.

DIET
Mainly benthic
amphipods,
filtered from
bottom
sediment; also
midwater fish
and crustaceans.

BREEDING
Calves every 2–3
years; gestation
12–13 months.

By the time the gray whale was being
given official protection, in the late 1930s,
it was already extinct in the North Atlantic
and was dangerously close to extinction in
the North Pacific. It is unclear why the
population in the North Atlantic had
disappeared a few hundred years earlier,
but whaling in the North Pacific was so
intense that it left no more than a few
hundred survivors. Fortunately, there
were just enough for the gray whale to
make a remarkable comeback—so
remarkable, in fact, that its recovery is
unmatched by any other species of great
whale. The current population of some
26,000 Californian gray whales may even
exceed pre-exploitation levels. However,
the population in the western North
Pacific is still critically endangered, with
as few as 100 animals remaining.
Once dubbed the devilfish by
whalers, for their ferocity in the
face of danger, gray whales
are better known
these days for
their friendly
behavior and curious
approaches to boats.

Where to look
Gray whales are found
only in the North Pacific. The eastern
population (Californian stock) migrates
on average about 5,000 miles between its

summer feeding grounds in the Arctic's Bering, Chukchi and western Beaufort seas and its winter breeding grounds around Baja California, Mexico. The western population (Korean stock) spends the summer in the Sea of Okhotsk and is believed to breed in tropical waters off southern China.

INCREDIBLE JOURNEYS OF THE GRAY WHALE

Gray whales are inveterate travelers, commuting along the entire length of the North American coastline, and back again, every year. The round-trip distance between their winter breeding grounds in Baja California, Mexico, and their summer feeding grounds in the Bering Sea can be as many as 12,500 miles, making their journey one of the longest migrations of any mammal population as a whole. The migration north tends to be close to shore and in good weather, the one south often takes place in stormier weather and is usually a little farther offshore (although still within sight of land).

Feeding in the Arctic: April—October

The vast majority of gray whales spend every summer in the Bering, Chukchi, and western Beaufort seas where, for about five months of the year, they eat as much as they possibly can. Feeding in relatively shallow water, they use their mouths like vacuum cleaners and literally suck up sediment from the seabed. They sieve this with their baleen plates, and then swallow the tiny crustaceans trapped inside. Each adult gray whale eats nearly 70 tons of these little creatures in one summer-long feast. Their aim is to put on enough body weight, in the form of blubber and fat, to survive the rest of the year without food.

Migrating south: November—February

Early in October, the Arctic weather begins to worsen and the whales prepare themselves to leave. Their migration south is organized like a military maneuver: the pregnant females are first to go, followed by nonpregnant females, then mature males, immature females next, and finally, the immature males. Over a period of several months, they file through Unimak Pass, a narrow gap between islands in the Aleutian chain, and head south. By the second week of January, huge numbers are passing southern California. With hardly a break, they average about 78 miles a day, and the entire journey takes them a couple of months.

Breeding in the subtropics: December—April

The pregnant females are the first to arrive in the breeding lagoons along the Pacific coast of Baja California. They give birth to their calves in the shallow backwaters while many of the other whales are still on their way south. The calves drink huge quantities of their mothers' fat-laden milk and gain weight rapidly. It is a race against time, because within a few months they will have to be fit and ready for their first journey north.

Migrating north: February—June

The gray whales tend to swim a little more slowly on their journey north (perhaps 43–60 miles a day) and the females with calves, especially, rest for a few hours or even a few days at a time. Funneling back into the Bering Sea, through Unimak Pass, they fan out across their Arctic feeding grounds for another summer. It will only be a few months before they are ready to leave once again and, as one yearly cycle comes to an end, another begins.

Southern Right Whale

Eubalaena australis

ID FACT FILE

OTHER NAMES
Black right whale.

MAXIMUM LENGTH
56 feet.

MAXIMUM WEIGHT
90 tons.

FIELD ID
Black with irregular white patches on underside; broad back with no fin; large head covered in callosities; strongly arched mouthline; large paddle-shaped flippers; V-shaped blow; usually raises flukes when diving.

DIET
Mainly copepods (which are so small about 8,000 would fit in a teaspoon); occasionally krill.

BREEDING
Calves every 3–5 years; gestation 12 months.

With their enormous heads covered in strange-looking callosities (hardened patches of skin), their dark, rotund bodies, and their lack of a dorsal fin, northern and southern right whales look almost identical. But they have long been considered distinct species and this separation has recently been supported by genetic evidence. Southern right whales have been studied since 1970—longer than any other baleen whale—when Roger Payne began to recognize individuals by the shape and pattern of their callosities in Peninsula Valdés, Argentina. Right whales are particularly active at the surface and can often be seen breaching, lobtailing, spyhopping, and even sailing (they raise flukes in the air and then sail downwind before swimming back to the starting point for another sail). Their mating system is unusual among whales because it is heavily dependent on sperm competition (male right whales have the largest testes in the animal kingdom—weighing nearly a ton) rather than competition between individuals.

Where to look

The southern right whale has a circumpolar
distribution in the southern hemisphere. It breeds in
South America, southern Africa, and Australasia
(and off several remote offshore islands such as
Crozet and Kerguelen). Its summer feeding grounds
are in colder waters around Antarctica and
elsewhere in the Southern Ocean. Exploited heavily
during the nineteenth century, its numbers now
appear to be recovering well.

Northern Right Whale

Eubalaena glacialis (North Atlantic)

Eubalaena japonica (North Pacific)

ID FACT FILE

OTHER NAMES
Black right
whale, Biscayan
right whale,
Nordkaper.

MAXIMUM LENGTH
59 feet.

MAXIMUM WEIGHT
100 tons.

FIELD ID
Black with
irregular white
patches on
underside; broad
back with no fin;
large head
covered in
callosities;
strongly arched
mouthline; large
paddle-shaped
flippers; V-
shaped blow;
usually raises
flukes when
diving.

DIET
Mainly copepods
(which are so
small about
8,000 would fit
in a teaspoon);
occasionally krill.

BREEDING
Calves every 3–5
years; gestation
12 months.

Recent genetic evidence suggests that there are two species of northern right whale, instead of just one, and that they have been evolving separately for millennia. However, they look virtually identical with their raised and roughened patches of skin, known as callosities. These occur on the whales in approximately the same places as facial hair on human males and, although they are black, usually appear white or orangey white due to massive infestations of whale lice. Callosities are found on both sexes and young calves, but their purpose is unknown. Northern right whales are the rarest large whales in the world and have never recovered from years of heavy exploitation by whalers. There are only about 300 North Atlantic right whales surviving today. Estimates for North Pacific right whales are less precise, but there are probably fewer than 100 left in the eastern population (just one calf has been seen here in the past century) and possibly a few hundred in the western population.

Where to look
The largest population is in the western North Atlantic—mainly off Cape Cod in spring, the Bay of Fundy off Canada and the Scotia Shelf (the continental shelf waters off Nova Scotia) in summer, and on breeding grounds off Florida and Georgia in winter. There are very occasional sightings in European waters. Small numbers survive in the North Pacific, mainly from the Sea of Okhotsk east to the Gulf of Alaska, with occasional sightings off the United States and Baja California.

NORTHERN RIGHT WHALES: ON THE VERGE OF EXTINCTION

North Atlantic right whales were probably the first whales to be hunted commercially: Basque whalers were killing them in the Bay of Biscay, north of Spain, as early as the eleventh century. The whales were killed primarily for their oil, which was distributed throughout Europe, but the Basques found a market for almost every part of their catch and even the excrement was used (for dyeing fabrics red). The whaling had spread to eastern Canada by 1530 and to New England by the 1600s and right whales continued to be popular targets for commercial whalers for many centuries. Whaling of North Pacific right whales began considerably later, in the Gulf of Alaska in 1835, but was no less intensive.

Named for being the "right" whales to catch, they were easy to approach, slow swimmers, lived close to shore, normally floated when dead, and provided large quantities of valuable oil, meat, and baleen (whalebone). By the early 1900s, tens or even hundreds of thousands of them had been killed, and all three species were critically close to extinction.

All populations of the right whale worldwide were protected from commercial whaling in the late 1930s, although some were killed illegally by Japan, Brazil, and the Soviet Union well into the 1950s and 1960s. But even after decades of international legal protection, only the southern right whale is showing signs of recovery.

Although the whaling has ceased, North Atlantic right whales are now threatened by heavy shipping and entanglement in commercial fishing gear. Between 1970 and 1999, no fewer than 16 were known to have been killed in collisions with ships (and two others probably died of their injuries), while three are known to have drowned in fishing nets and a further eight were seriously injured and probably died too. When the surviving population is so small, these are significant numbers. The sad fact is that northern right whales are among the world's most critically endangered mammals and are probably closer to extinction than any other large whale.

Pygmy Right Whale
Caperea marginata

ID FACT FILE

OTHER NAMES
None.

MAXIMUM LENGTH
21 feet.

MAXIMUM WEIGHT
3.4 tons.

FIELD ID
Quite small and sleek; gray upperside, paler underside; pronounced falcate fin; may be twin chevrons on back and sides; strongly arched mouth-line; no callo-sities on head; indistinct blow; undemonstrative behavior; rarely raises flukes when diving.

DIET
Probably copepods, but also some krill.

BREEDING
Calving interval and gestation period unknown.

The pygmy right whale is the smallest species of baleen whale and one of the cetaceans known least well. Our knowledge is based on fewer than 20 sightings at sea and a few dozen dead animals caught by fishermen or washed ashore. Like the other right whales it has a strongly arched lower jaw, but it differs from them in having a pronounced dorsal fin and no callosities. It is the only baleen whale that has not been the target of large-scale commercial whaling and the only known threat is occasional drownings in fishing nets off South Africa. Pygmy right whales are usually seen alone or in pairs, although large aggregations of as many as 80 individuals have been recorded. Virtually nothing is known about their social structure or behavior. Unless it is possible to see the distinctive arched mouthline, they can be very difficult to distinguish from dwarf and Antarctic minke whales at sea.

Where to look

The pygmy right whale is known from a small number of widely dispersed records across temperate waters of the southern hemisphere (never south of the Antarctic Convergence). It has been recorded mainly in Australasia, South Africa, South America, and a few islands in between.

Bowhead Whale

Balaena mysticetus

ID FACT FILE

OTHER NAMES
Greenland right whale, Greenland whale, Arctic right whale, Arctic whale.

MAXIMUM LENGTH
66 feet.

MAXIMUM WEIGHT
90 tons.

FIELD ID
Black, rotund body; no fin; irregular white patch on chin with black spots; two distinct humps in profile; huge head; strongly arched mouth; V-shaped blow; no callosities or barnacles; often raises flukes when diving.

DIET
Mainly krill and copepods, but also other invertebrates.

BREEDING
Calves every 3–4 years; gestation probably 13–14 months.

The only large whale found exclusively in the Arctic, the bowhead is well adapted to life in its freezing home. With a layer of blubber up to 20 inches thick, and an ability to create its own breathing holes by breaking through ice up to six feet thick, it is able to live in higher latitudes than any other baleen whale. Its distinctive head is almost triangular in profile and, when lying at the surface, forms the first of two humps (the second is the back) that make it resemble the shape of the Loch Ness Monster. There is growing evidence that, like humpback whales, bowhead males produce songs that may advertise for females. Heavily hunted by commercial whalers for several centuries, and still being taken by small-scale indigenous whalers, the bowhead is not particularly common. The total number of survivors is estimated to be only 8,000–9,000, and most of these live in a single population in the Bering, Chukchi, and Beaufort Seas. The remaining four recognized populations are highly endangered.

Where to look

Bowhead whales are found in cold waters around the Arctic and subarctic, rarely far from the pack ice. They normally migrate to the high Arctic in spring and summer, as the sea ice breaks up and recedes, and then retreat southward with the advancing ice edge in fall and winter.

Humpback Whale
Megaptera novaeangliae

ID FACT FILE

OTHER NAMES
Hump-backed
whale.
MAXIMUM LENGTH
56 feet.
MAXIMUM WEIGHT
40 tons.
FIELD ID
Stocky body;
black upperside,
white, black, or
mottled
underside; low,
stubby fin often
on a hump;
extremely long
flippers white
below and white
or black (North
Pacific) above;
single, bushy
blow; variable
black-and-white
fluke pattern;
often raises
flukes when
diving.

DIET
Krill and variety
of small
schooling fish.
BREEDING
Calves every
2–3 years;
gestation about
12 months.

The humpback whale is relatively well
studied, yet many aspects of its life are
still shrouded in mystery and we are only
just beginning to unravel some of its
best-kept secrets. It is well known for its
long flippers, which can grow to nearly
one-third of its body length and give the
humpback its scientific name. *Megaptera
novaeangliae* means "big-winged New
Englander," New England being where
the first specimen was described. Its
head is also distinctive, with a series of
knobs or tubercles covering the rostrum
and much of the lower jaw; about the size
of a golf ball, each knob is a hair follicle
with a single, coarse hair growing out of
its center. Humpbacks are among the
most energetic of all the large whales and
are well known for their spectacular
breaching, as well as lobtailing, flipper-

slapping, and spyhopping. Even when they seem to be resting, they are fun to watch and may lie on their backs or sides, holding their enormous flippers high in the air.

Where to look

Widely distributed from the poles to the tropics, humpbacks feed in cool waters during spring and summer and breed in warmer water during the winter. Individual humpbacks migrate farther than most other cetaceans—making a round-trip journey of up to 9,950 miles. Nearly a quarter of a million were killed by commercial whalers, but they seem to be making a good recovery in many parts of their range.

FISHING WITH NETS OF BUBBLES

Humpback whales have developed an extraordinarily diverse and ingenious range of techniques for catching their food. They lunge through patches of fish or krill with their mouths wide open, literally gulping vast mouthfuls out of the ocean, and even stun their prey with slaps of their flippers or flukes.

But no fishing technique is more impressive than fishing with bubbles. Many humpbacks use huge, explosive bubble clouds, releasing a single blast up to 66 feet across that probably concentrates and disorientates their prey. But to catch herring in the northern North Pacific and Bering Sea they prefer more delicate bubble nets, which strongly resemble manmade seine nets both in design and in the way they are deployed.

Known simply as "bubble-netting," this particular fishing technique is all the more sensational because the climax of the action takes place in full view above the surface of the water.

When a humpback whale forms a bubble net on its own, it dives beneath a school of fish and starts to release bubbles from its blowholes. Then it swims slowly toward the surface, in a spiral, to form a circular barrier of bubbles around the school. As soon as the "net" is complete, it swims through the center with its mouth wide open. The water is flushed out through the baleen plates, as the whale rises above the surface, and the fish trapped inside its mouth are swept up by the tongue and swallowed.

Incredibly, as many as 20 humpback whales may work together in a more complex form of bubble-net fishing, requiring an almost incomprehensible level of coordination.

It begins with all the members of a fishing group swimming slowly at the surface, spending a few minutes resting and catching their collective breath. Then they all dive and disappear beneath the surface together. No one knows exactly how they organize themselves underwater but, after about five or 10 minutes, bubbles begin to break the surface, each one roughly the size of a dinner plate. These form part of a huge circle that can be up to 150 feet across. Suddenly, hundreds of tons of blubber and gaping mouths erupt from within the circle in one great foaming mass. With water gushing down their distended throat pleats, and fish leaping for their lives, the whales explode to a height of nearly 20 feet before sinking back into the depths. It is one of the greatest wildlife spectacles on Earth.

Opposite: Lunge-feeding humpback whale, south-east Alaska

SINGING HUMPBACKS

Drop a hydrophone into the water in an area where humpback whales are breeding and you may hear a baffling medley of moans, groans, roars, snores, squeaks, and whistles. These are the unearthly, hauntingly beautiful sounds made by male humpback whales, which are famous for singing the longest and most complex songs in the animal kingdom.

The singing whales hang almost upside down in the water, often fairly close to the surface. With their eyes closed and their heads pointing toward the seabed, they sometimes wave their enormous flippers up and down like conductors in front of an orchestra.

Humpback whale, Silver Bank, Dominican Republic

No one knows exactly how they sing. They have no vocal chords and, intriguingly, while they are in full song, no air is released. They do not even open their mouths. The latest theory is that they shift air around inside their bodies, but much more research is needed before it is possible to be sure of the details.

They sing throughout the day and night—and may continue for 24 hours or even longer with hardly a break. Because most of the singing takes place at the breeding grounds, and exclusively by males, it is probably used to woo females and to warn away unwanted competition from rival males. But it is also possible that the songs have more subtle meanings and nuances that we do not yet understand.

A song can last for as long as half an hour and, as soon as the whale has finished, it simply goes back to the beginning and sings the same song all over again. Each song consists of several main components, or phrases, which are always sung in the same order and are repeated a number of times but are forever being refined and improved. This means that the song heard one day is quite different to the one being heard several months later. When the whales return to their breeding grounds the following winter, they immediately start singing the version of the song that was in vogue at the end of the previous breeding season.

Even more extraordinary is the fact that all the humpbacks in one area sing broadly the same song, incorporating each other's improvisations as they go along. It is as if they compose and then rewrite the "music" together. In this way, the entire composition changes over a period of several years.

Meanwhile, humpback whales in other oceans sing very different compositions. They probably all croon about the same trials and tribulations in life, but it is as if the ones living around Hawaii sing in American English, while those living off the coast of the Dominican Republic, for example, sing in Caribbean English. The differences are so distinctive that experts can tell where a whale was recorded simply by listening to the intricacies of its own special dialect.

Common Minke Whale

Balaenoptera acutorostrata

ID FACT FILE

OTHER NAMES
Little finner, little piked whale, pikehead, lesser finback, lesser rorqual.

MAXIMUM LENGTH
35 feet.

MAXIMUM WEIGHT
9 tons.

FIELD ID
Small and sleek; dark upperside, white underside; sharply-pointed snout; snout breaks surface first; falcate fin; white bands on flippers in many populations; indistinct or invisible blow; does not raise flukes when diving.

DIET
Mainly small schooling fish and krill.

BREEDING
Calves every 1–2 years; gestation about 10 months.

The common minke is the second-smallest baleen whale, after the pygmy right, and is also the most common. Reputedly named after a novice eighteenth-century Norwegian whaler, named Meincke, it is a frequent sight on whale-watching trips in many parts of the world. Surprisingly little is known about many aspects of its life, though, and limited evidence suggests an intriguingly complex social structure with populations segregated by age, sex, or reproductive condition. Minkes are quite variable in appearance. Animals in the northern hemisphere, for example, have a white band on their flippers, but this extends into a white shoulder patch or is absent on many southern hemisphere animals. Two subspecies are recognized—North Atlantic minke whale (*Balaenoptera acutorostrata acutorostrata*) and North Pacific minke whale (*Balaenoptera acutorostrata scammoni*)—and there may be a third, known as the dwarf minke whale for its smaller size, found only in the southern hemisphere. Minkes are curious and will approach boats.

Where to look

Found virtually worldwide from the tropics to the edge of the polar ice, mainly in warmer waters in winter and cooler waters in summer. The minke whale's small size saved it from commercial whalers until the twentieth century, but many tens of thousands have been killed in the last hundred years. It is still being hunted today, by Norway and Iceland in the North Atlantic and Japan in the North Pacific and the Antarctic.

Antarctic Minke Whale

Balaenoptera bonaerensis

ID FACT FILE

OTHER NAMES
Little finner, little piked whale, pikehead, lesser finback, lesser rorqual.

MAXIMUM LENGTH
35 feet.

MAXIMUM WEIGHT
9 tons.

FIELD ID
Small and sleek; dark upperside, white underside; asymmetrical baleen coloration; sharply-pointed snout; snout breaks surface first; falcate fin; flippers may be light colored but no white bands; indistinct or invisible blow; does not raise flukes when diving.

DIET
Mainly krill, but sometimes small schooling fish.

BREEDING
Calves every 1–2 years; gestation about 10 months.

A new species of minke whale, the Antarctic minke, was officially recognized in the late 1990s. It differs significantly from the common minke in many external and skeletal features (its baleen plates, for example, have an asymmetrical coloration) and the two species are so genetically different that they are more closely related to sei and Bryde's whales than they are to each other. However, they can be difficult to tell apart at sea. Antarctic minkes overlap in range with dwarf minkes (a smaller form of the common minke) but on average are almost a full seven feet longer. They are usually seen alone or in small groups, although larger gatherings are sometimes encountered on good feeding grounds. They are believed to form a significant part of the diet of Antarctic killer whales and are still being killed by Japan for the dubious purpose of scientific research. In the past century, whalers have killed more than 100,000 minke whales in the southern hemisphere and most of these were probably Antarctic minkes.

Where to look

As its name suggests, the Antarctic minke whale
spends summer in the cold waters around
Antarctica—from about 55°S through the deep
waters of the Southern Ocean and right up to the ice
edge. Little is known about its seasonal migrations,
but most individuals probably spend the winter
between about 7°S and 35°S. A few may reach as far
north as the equator.

Antarctic minke whales, Antarctic Peninsula

Bryde's Whale
Balaenoptera edeni

ID FACT FILE

OTHER NAMES
Tropical whale.
MAXIMUM LENGTH
51 feet.
MAXIMUM WEIGHT
40 tons.
FIELD ID
Dark, smoky gray
upperside, white
underside
(upperside may
appear brown in
some lights);
skin may be
mottled; three
parallel
longitudinal
ridges on head;
prominent,
falcate fin;
narrow, hazy
blow; arches
back but does
not raise flukes
when diving.
DIET
Mainly small
schooling fish,
but also krill.
BREEDING
Calves every 2
years; gestation
about 12
months.

Bryde's whale is named after a
Norwegian called Johan Bryde, who was
a whaling pioneer in South Africa. The
least known of the large baleen whales, it
is unusual because it does not seem to
migrate long distances between separate
feeding and breeding grounds every year.
It stays in warm waters, and may even eat
and breed in the same general area. In
the past Bryde's whales that were caught
by whalers were often mistakenly
recorded as sei whales, but they are
unique in having three longitudinal
ridges along the top of the head (all other
members of the family have just one).
The history of whaling for Bryde's whales
is largely unknown, because of the
confusion with sei whales, but in recent
years Japanese whalers have been taking
this species in the North Pacific. There
may be more than one species and,
indeed, it is likely that a pygmy form of
Bryde's whale will be assigned separate
species status in the near future.

Where to look

Bryde's whales are found in tropical to temperate waters worldwide. Rarely moving farther north or south than 40°, they occur both offshore and near the coast. There seem to be specific pockets of abundance where there is unusually high productivity, such as off southern Africa and western Australia. The pygmy form is known from the eastern Indian Ocean, the western Pacific, and Australasia, and may yet be found elsewhere.

Sei Whale
Balaenoptera borealis

ID FACT FILE

OTHER NAMES
Sardine whale, pollack whale, coalfish whale, Rudolphi's rorqual, finner.

MAXIMUM LENGTH
62 feet.

MAXIMUM WEIGHT
45 tons.

FIELD ID
Large, sleek body; dark gray upperside, white or creamy underside; often has oval-shaped scars; single longitudinal ridge on head; tall, falcate fin; tall columnar blow; does not arch back as much as other whales or raise flukes when diving.

DIET
Broad range of prey from small schooling fish to krill and copepods.

BREEDING
Calves every 2–3 years; gestation 11–12 months.

The sei whale is poorly known. It lives far from shore, tends to be elusive, and does not seem to gather in the same predictable areas year after year. There may be large numbers of sei whales in a particular region one year and then none for years or even decades afterward. For this reason no commercial whale-watching operation relies on this species, although it is sometimes encountered during tours specializing in humpbacks, minkes, and other large whales. Named after a Norwegian word for the fish we call pollack, because the appearance of pollack off Norway's coast sometimes coincided with the arrival of sei whales, it is capable of swimming at up to 25 knots, making it one of the fastest of the large whales. For many years it was confused with the similar Bryde's whale, but the two species can be told apart by the number of longitudinal ridges along the tops of their heads.

Where to look

Found worldwide from tropical to cool temperate
waters, most sei whales probably migrate between
cool summer feeding grounds and warm winter
breeding grounds. More than 200,000 were killed in
Antarctica in the past century and numbers there
remain greatly depleted. Unknown numbers were
killed elsewhere (whalers confused them with
Bryde's whales and anything vaguely resembling a
fin whale was often recorded merely as a "finner").
Seis appear to be reasonably abundant in the North
Atlantic and North Pacific.

Fin Whale

Balaenoptera physalus

ID FACT FILE

OTHER NAMES
Finback, finner, herring whale, common rorqual, razorback.

MAXIMUM LENGTH
89 feet.

MAXIMUM WEIGHT
120 tons.

FIELD ID
Exceptionally large and sleek; dark upperside, light underside; asymmetrical head pigmentation; grayish-white chevron; small, backward-sloping fin far down back; single longitudinal ridge on head; tall, narrow blow; rarely raises flukes when diving.

DIET
Schooling fish, krill and other crustaceans, some squid (mainly krill in southern hemisphere).

BREEDING
Calves every 2–3 years; gestation 11–12 months

The second-largest animal on Earth after the blue whale, the fin whale is a sleek and fast swimmer capable of reaching speeds of over 25 knots. It is unusual in having asymmetrical pigmentation on its head—the lower jaw, mouth cavity, and some of the baleen plates are white on the right side, but they are uniformly gray or black on the left side. No one knows the reason for such intriguing coloration, but it may be an adaptation to confuse the whale's small prey. Females are up to 10

percent longer than males and southern hemisphere animals can be 20 percent longer than their northern hemisphere counterparts. So the average length for a northern hemisphere male is 69 feet, while the average for a southern hemisphere female is 85 feet. Northern and southern hemisphere populations do not come into contact and may be separate subspecies. Male and female fin whales make very loud, low-frequency vocalizations that can travel over hundreds of miles in deep water.

Where to look

Found in tropical, temperate, and polar regions
worldwide, it is most common in cooler waters
offshore. Some populations seem to be resident all
year round, or make very short migrations, but
others travel between warm waters in winter and
cooler waters in summer. No distinct breeding or
calving grounds have been identified. The world
population was substantially reduced by commercial
whaling (three-quarters of a million were killed in
the southern hemisphere alone).

Blue Whale
Balaenoptera musculus

ID FACT FILE

OTHER NAMES
Sulfur-bottom,
Sibbald's rorqual,
great northern
rorqual.

MAXIMUM LENGTH
110 feet.

MAXIMUM WEIGHT
190 tons.

FIELD ID
Exceptionally
large; mottled
blue-gray; tiny,
stubby fin far
down back;
broad, flattened,
U-shaped head;
huge blowhole
splashguard;
single
longitudinal
ridge on head;
extremely thick
tailstock; very
tall blow; often
raises flukes
when diving.

The largest animal known to have lived
on Earth, the blue whale is almost as long
as a Boeing 737 and needs so much food
that, in terms of weight, it could eat a
fully grown African elephant every day.
But its sheer size made it one of the most
sought-after species during the heyday of
whaling and it was hunted relentlessly
from the late nineteenth century until
beyond the middle of the twentieth
century. No fewer than 360,000 were
killed in Antarctic waters alone. Some
populations were reduced by 99 percent
of their original numbers and it is likely
that they will never recover. Blue whales
possess the loudest voice in the animal
kingdom, emitting low-frequency sounds
that can travel literally hundreds of miles
in deep water. It is not known whether
these are for long-distance

DIET
Mainly krill,
occasionally
pelagic crabs.

BREEDING
Calves every 2–3
years; gestation
about 11
months.

communication or to assist with navigation and orientation. There is a subspecies known as the pygmy blue whale, which is particularly common in the Indian Ocean and may ultimately be recognized as a separate species.

Where to look

Worldwide from the tropics to the poles, although its distribution is very patchy. Some populations migrate long distances between low-latitude winter breeding grounds and high-latitude summer feeding grounds, but others appear to be resident. The only population that may be thriving today summers off the coasts of California and Mexico.

Sperm Whale
Physeter catodon

ID FACT FILE

OTHER NAMES
Cachalot, great
sperm whale.
Latin name
*Physeter
macrocephalus*
is also
applicable.

MAXIMUM LENGTH
36 feet (female),
59 feet (male).

MAXIMUM WEIGHT
24 tons (female),
57 tons (male).

FIELD ID
Dark body with
wrinkled skin;
huge, squarish
head; low hump
instead of fin;
"knuckles" from
hump to flukes;
single, slitlike
blowhole;
sideways,
forward-angled
blow; often lies
stationary at
surface; raises
flukes high when
diving.

DIET
Mainly squid, but
also octopuses,
sharks, and
other fish.

BREEDING
Calves every 4–6
years (longer in
older females);
gestation 14–18
months.

With its disproportionately large head and wrinkled skin, the sperm whale is very distinctive. The largest of the toothed whales, it dives deeper and for longer than any other cetacean (with the possible exception of some beaked whales). No other cetacean shows such a marked difference in size between the sexes—males are almost twice as large as females and lead very different lives. Groups of females and immatures of both sexes stay in the same general area for many years, but adult males are generally solitary and travel huge distances. In fact, the males travel so far and wide that populations around the world are very similar genetically. The sperm whale was the mainstay of the whaling industry for many years, hunted mainly for its spermaceti oil (a waxy oil found in the head) and body oil. It is believed that more than a million sperm whales were killed over several centuries and the latest population estimate suggests there could be as few as 360,000 left.

Where to look

Distribution is patchy worldwide from the tropics to high latitudes near the edge of the pack ice. Sperm whales are most common offshore and over deepwater canyons, but can be found close to shore if the water is sufficiently deep. Most females and immature males live in temperate and tropical seas at latitudes less than 40° (50° in the North Pacific). Only the large adult males venture to the extreme north and south of the range, where they feed.

THE WHALE THAT THINKS IT IS A SUBMARINE

Sperm whales behave more like submarines than air-breathing mammals. Capable of diving well beyond the limits of almost any other mammal, they disappear into the cold, dark ocean depths to catch deepwater squid or sharks and other large fish.

They eat as much as a ton of food every day, each prey animal ranging in size from a few inches to almost the length of the whales themselves. One individual was observed tackling a giant squid some 48 feet long, including its tentacles, while no fewer than 28,000 smaller squid were found in the stomach of another.

Scientists from the Woods Hole Oceanographic Institute recorded an incredible, record-breaking dive during a research study near the Caribbean island of Dominica. In 1991, they tagged a pair of male sperm whales and regularly tracked them at depths of 1,300–2,000 feet. On one occasion, though, the larger of the two whales made a breathtaking dive to a depth of 6,560 feet.

There is plenty of circumstantial evidence to suggest that sperm whales may be able to dive even deeper. On August 25, 1969, for example, a male sperm whale was killed by whalers 99 miles south of Durban, South Africa. Inside its

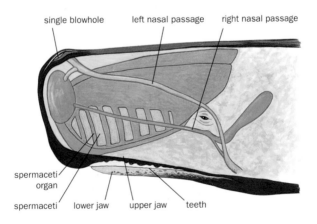

single blowhole   left nasal passage   right nasal passage

spermaceti organ

spermaceti   lower jaw   upper jaw   teeth

stomach were two small sharks which, according to local
experts, had been swallowed about an hour earlier; these
were later identified as a particular kind of dogfish, found
only on the seafloor. Since the water in that area exceeds a
depth of 10,475 feet for a radius of some 30–40 miles, it is
logical to assume that the sperm whale had been to a similar
depth when hunting the two sharks.

Incidentally, the same whale also made one of the longest
confirmed dives of any mammal. By the time it surfaced to
breathe, having caught its prey, it had been underwater for an
incredible one hour 52 minutes.

One explanation for such astonishing diving capabilities
may lie in the sperm whale's enormous, barrel-shaped head.
Much of the bulk of the head consists of a strange spongy
tissue, known as the spermaceti organ, which is saturated
with a yellowy wax. According to one theory, this could be
used to control the whale's buoyancy in the water. By altering
the temperature (and thus the density) of the wax the whale
could sink or float with the minimum of effort. Another idea
is that it cushions the animal's head during fights (heavy
scarring and occasional broken teeth and jaws suggest serious
skirmishes between males). But the most likely theory to
explain the purpose of this massive oil-filled organ is that it
works as an acoustic lens to channel sound emissions.

Dwarf Sperm Whale

Kogia sima

ID FACT FILE

OTHER NAMES
Owen's pygmy
sperm whale.

MAXIMUM LENGTH
9 feet.

MAXIMUM WEIGHT
606 pounds.

FIELD ID
Small, robust
body; bluish-gray
upperside, dull
white or pinkish
underside;
squarish head
with underslung
lower jaw;
prominent,
falcate fin
midway along
back; false
"gill"; low,
inconspicuous
blow; floats
motionless at
surface; does
not raise flukes
when diving.

DIET
Mainly mid- and
deep-water
squid, some fish
and crustaceans.

BREEDING
May calve every
2 years or less;
gestation about
12 months.

Like their much larger and better-known relative, dwarf sperm whales have spermaceti organs in their heads and are deep divers. They are very similar in appearance to pygmy sperm whales and the two species are difficult to tell apart at sea, except in perfect conditions at very close range. They were separated as distinct species as recently as 1996, but *Kogia sima* was named one hundred years earlier, in 1866. The dwarf sperm whale is slightly smaller (by about 18 inches on average) and usually has a more prominent dorsal fin positioned farther forward on the back. Stranded individuals of both species have been mistaken for sharks because of their underslung lower jaws and the distinctive crescent-shaped markings on either side of the head between the eye and the flipper (which resemble gill-slits and have been dubbed "false gills"). Dwarf sperm whales occur alone or in small groups of up to 10 animals of mixed age and sex. Both species are often seen lying motionless at the surface, with the back of the head exposed and the tail hanging down in the water. It is possible to approach them quite closely, but they then startle and dive.

Where to look

Dwarf sperm whales are found worldwide in tropical to temperate waters of the Atlantic, Pacific, and Indian oceans, although they have never been officially recorded across vast areas within this assumed range. Some evidence suggests that the dwarf sperm whale may prefer warmer, shallower coastal waters than the pygmy sperm whale. There is no evidence that the species migrates.

Pygmy Sperm Whale
Kogia breviceps

ID FACT FILE

OTHER NAMES
Lesser sperm whale, short-headed sperm whale, lesser cachalot.

MAXIMUM LENGTH
12 feet 6 inches.

MAXIMUM WEIGHT
992 pounds.

FIELD ID
Small, robust body; bluish-gray upperside, dull white or pinkish underside; squarish head with underslung lower jaw; falcate fin behind midline on body; false "gill"; low, inconspicuous blow; floats motionless at surface; does not raise flukes when diving.

DIET
Mainly mid- and deep-water squid, some fish and crustaceans.

BREEDING
May calve every 2 years or less; gestation about 12 months.

Like the virtually identical dwarf sperm whale, the pygmy sperm whale is rarely encountered at sea except in a few well known hotspots. Neither species appears to be particularly numerous, although they can be overlooked in anything but the calmest conditions and may be more common than the lack of evidence currently suggests. Both species are sometimes killed in Japan, Indonesia, and the Lesser Antilles, and at least some are drowned in fishing nets. They are unusual among cetaceans in having a store of dark reddish-brown liquid in the lower intestines, which they expel into the water when they are startled—perhaps as a decoy, like the ink of a squid. They also have unusually-shaped heads, which appear square from the side and conical when viewed from above or below; they become blunter and squarer as the animals age. Pygmy sperm whales occur alone or in small groups of up to six animals of mixed age and sex.

Where to look
Pygmy sperm whales are found worldwide in tropical to temperate waters of the Atlantic, Pacific, and Indian oceans, though they have never been officially recorded across vast areas within this assumed range. Limited evidence suggests that the pygmy sperm whale prefers cooler, deeper waters seaward of the continental shelf. There is no evidence that the species migrates.

Narwhal

Monodon monoceros

ID FACT FILE

OTHER NAMES
Narwhale.

MAXIMUM LENGTH
15 feet.

MAXIMUM WEIGHT
1.6 tons.

FIELD ID
Long tusk of male; mottled black-and-white back and sides; low fleshy ridge instead of fin; short, rounded head; slight hint of beak; short, upcurled flippers; convex "backward-facing" flukes; inhabits very high latitudes; rarely raises flukes when diving.

DIET
Variety of fish, squid and crustaceans.

BREEDING
Calves every 2–3 years; gestation about 15 months.

Centuries ago the male narwhal's long, spiraling tusk was believed to be the horn of the legendary unicorn and traders selling it made huge profits by keeping this distinctive whale's existence a secret. Looking like a gnarled and twisted walking stick, the tusk is actually a modified tooth—the left of two upper teeth, it pierces the lip and keeps growing to a length of up to 10 feet. A small number of males have two tusks and, rarely, females grow them as well. Their purpose is still a matter of debate, but they are certainly not used to spear fish and may instead be weapons in fights over females or used as visual displays of strength. Narwhals are deep divers, capable of staying underwater for as long as 20 minutes and reaching depths of more than 3,300 feet. They have been hunted for centuries by indigenous peoples for their meat and tusks and in some areas are threatened by oil and gas exploration and pollution. The total population is believed to be around 50,000.

Where to look

A truly Arctic species, the narwhal lives farther north than almost any other cetacean. Found mostly above the Arctic Circle, and right to the edge of the permanent ice, it moves with the receding and expanding ice edge. It is most common on the North Atlantic side of the Arctic (especially Greenland and northwestern Canada) and less common on the North Pacific side.

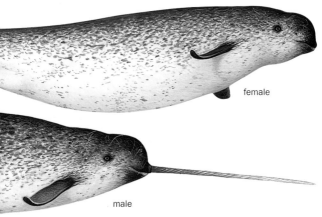

female

male

Beluga
Delphinapterus leucas

ID FACT FILE

OTHER NAMES
Belukha, sea
canary, white
whale.
MAXIMUM LENGTH
16 feet.
MAXIMUM WEIGHT
1.6 tons.
FIELD ID
White adult body
color; small head
with rounded
melon; flexible
neck; narrow
dorsal ridge
instead of fin;
extremely short
beak; broad
mouthline; dark
fringes to ridge,
flippers, and
flukes; frequently
spyhops; no
acrobatics; high
latitudes.
DIET
Variety of fish,
squid,
octopuses,
crustaceans, and
marine worms.
BREEDING
Calves every 3
years; gestation
about 11–14
months.

Ancient mariners used to call the beluga the "sea canary" because of its great repertoire of trills, moos, clicks, squeaks, and twitters, which was once described by a beluga scientist as sounding like a string orchestra tuning up before a concert. One of the most vocal of all the toothed whales, it can even be heard from above the surface. Unlike most other cetaceans, it can change the shape of its extraordinary bulging head and is able to turn its head from side to side or move it up and down. Not all belugas are white: the body color changes with age, from dark slate-gray at birth to pure white (with dark lines along the dorsal ridge and the edges of the flippers and flukes) in adulthood. Known to dive to depths of at least 2,625 feet, belugas are believed to forage near the seabed. They have been hunted for centuries and pollution is a serious threat in some regions. The best population estimate is around 100,000.

Where to look

Belugas are found only in seasonally ice-covered waters of the subarctic and Arctic. They occur mostly in shallow coastal waters, but will enter estuaries and even rivers. The largest population (accounting for 40 percent of the total) lives in the Beaufort Sea, but they are more readily seen in eastern Canada's lower St. Lawrence River and the Churchill River in western Hudson Bay.

BEAKED WHALES

The beaked whales are the strangest and least known of all the cetaceans. Several of them have never been seen alive and the only evidence of their existence has been gleaned from dead animals caught by fishermen or washed ashore. Others are known from just a few brief encounters at sea, but have never been photographed. Very few have been studied in any detail.

There are currently 21 known species, all belonging to the family Ziphiidae. But this figure is constantly under review as new species are discovered and described. The most recent addition to the list is Perrin's beaked whale, which was formally named in 2002 and is known from just five animals stranded along the coast of California. Another relatively new species is Bahamonde's beaked whale, which was added to the list in 1995. Also known as the spade-toothed whale, this whale was described from nothing more than part of a skull found in the Juan Fernández Islands, off the coast of Chile.

Beaked whales are small- to medium-sized whales, ranging in length from just over 13 feet to nearly 43 feet. As their name suggests, the majority of them have pronounced beaks, which are relatively shorter than in most dolphins but longer than in most whales. They also have a pair of distinctive throat grooves (in the shape of a "V") and, unique among cetaceans, slight depressions called "flipper pockets" where their small flippers can be tucked away alongside the body.

But their most remarkable feature is their teeth. There are no functional teeth in females or immature males (they do not erupt or are absent altogether) and there are only two or four functional teeth in the lower jaw of adult males. Shepherd's beaked whale is the main exception: both sexes have a full set of normal odontocete teeth in both the upper and lower jaws. Also, tiny teeth are present in the upper jaw of both sexes in Gray's beaked whales (embedded in the gum rather than the bone).

Observing and identifying beaked whales at sea can be extremely difficult. They usually live far from land and spend relatively little time at the surface between dives. More frustratingly, many species look remarkably alike from a distance. Relying on color alone is virtually impossible for most species, since so little is known about the coloration of live animals and the little we do know suggests that there is tremendous variation between individuals. Normally there is

no visible blow, and no beaked whales are known to lift their flukes when diving. In many cases, females are impossible to identify positively at sea unless they are accompanied by males.

However, more researchers have made an effort to study the enigmatic beaked whales in recent years and, although they are still shrouded in mystery, our knowledge has improved enormously.

Peruvian beaked whale skull

Sowerby's Beaked Whale

Mesoplodon bidens

ID FACT FILE

OTHER NAMES
North Sea beaked whale, North Atlantic beaked whale.

MAXIMUM LENGTH
18 feet.

MAXIMUM WEIGHT
1.3 tons.

FIELD ID
(Male only). Bluish-gray or slate-gray upperside, lighter underside; teeth midway along long, slender beak; slight bulge in front of blowhole; small falcate fin two-thirds of the way along back; limited scarring; usually unobtrusive behavior; surfaces at steep angle.

DIET
Squid and some fish.

BREEDING
Calving interval and gestation period unknown.

Sowerby's beaked whale was the first of the beaked whales to be described—a male stranded in 1800 in the Moray Firth, northeastern Scotland, and the skull was collected. A couple of years later, James Sowerby, an English watercolor artist, painted a picture of the skull and how he imagined the animal might have looked. Although its existence has been known for more than two centuries, Sowerby's beaked whale is rarely encountered at sea and is still poorly known. It does occasionally strand, but basic natural history data such as stomach contents is still limited. The position of the teeth in the male is distinctive, lying midway between the tip of the beak and the corner of the

female

mouth, although they may be visible only at close range. Females are probably unidentifiable at sea. They are usually seen alone or in small groups of up to 10 animals of mixed sex and age and are capable of diving for at least half an hour.

Where to look
With one of the most northerly distributions of all beaked whales, this species is found mainly in cold temperate and subarctic waters of the northern North Atlantic. It appears to be most common in the east, especially in the northern North Sea. There are no known hunts, although Sowerby's beaked whale has been hunted in the past off Iceland and in the Barents Sea. Nothing is known about its abundance.

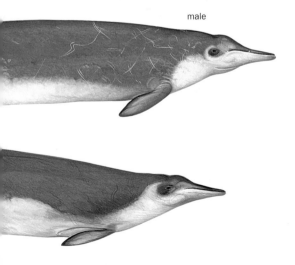

male

Andrews' Beaked Whale

Mesoplodon bowdoini

ID FACT FILE

OTHER NAMES
Bowdoin's beaked whale, splay-toothed beaked whale, deepcrest beaked whale.

MAXIMUM LENGTH
16 feet.

MAXIMUM WEIGHT
Possibly 1.5 tons.

FIELD ID
(Male only). Robust body; dark blue-black color; white scratches and scars; short, thick beak predominantly white; strongly arched mouthline; teeth visible in middle of beak; small fin.

DIET
Probably squid and some fish.

BREEDING
Calving interval and gestation period unknown.

Andrews' beaked whale is so similar in appearance and morphology to Hubbs' beaked whale that it has been suggested they belong to the same species. However, based on genetic evidence they are currently considered to be distinct species. Andrews' has never been

male

positively identified at sea, so everything we know about it has been inferred from strandings. These tend to occur infrequently, suggesting that it is relatively rare. The male, in particular, is rather distinctive with a short, thick beak and a large tooth perched on the top of each side of its highly arched lower jaw. Linear body scarring on adult males is probably made by the teeth of other males. The common name refers to the describer, a curator at the American Museum of Natural History in New York, Roy Chapman Andrews.

Where to look

It is known only from strandings along the southern coast of Australia (including Tasmania) and New Zealand (including some subantarctic islands), as well as oceanic islands such as the Falkland Islands and Tristan da Cunha. Such limited evidence suggests that Andrews' beaked whale has a circumpolar distribution in the southern hemisphere north of the Antarctic Convergence.

Hubbs' Beaked Whale
Mesoplodon carlhubbsi

Hubbs' beaked whale is another poorly-known member of the family and, again, most information comes from strandings. Adult males are covered in a remarkable number of single and double linear scars, which are probably made by the teeth of other males during aggressive encounters over females or dominance hierarchies. Other male beaked whales have similar scarring, but rarely as much as in this species. It is so similar in appearance and morphology to Andrews' beaked whale

ID FACT FILE

OTHER NAMES
Arch-beaked whale.
MAXIMUM LENGTH
17 feet.
MAXIMUM WEIGHT
1.5 tons.
FIELD ID
(Male only). Dark, robust body; tangle of linear scars; raised white "cap" on fairly bulbous melon; stocky, elongated beak mainly white; strongly arched lower jaw; massive teeth visible on top of arch in centre of beak; slightly falcate fin.
DIET
Squid and some fish.
BREEDING
Calving interval and gestation period unknown.

male

that it has been suggested they belong to the same species. However, based on genetic evidence, they are currently considered to be distinct. Hubbs' beaked whale was named after the American ichthyologist Carl Hubbs. In 1945, a live specimen stranded outside his office at Scripps Institution of Oceanography in California.

Where to look
Known only from temperate waters in the North Pacific, Hubbs' beaked whale appears to be most common along the California coast and north into British Columbia. It may occur as far south as the Pacific coast of Baja California, Mexico. However, it has also been recorded in Japan (along the northeastern coast of the main island of Honshu) and therefore may range right across the North Pacific.

Blainville's Beaked Whale

Mesoplodon densirostris

ID FACT FILE

OTHER NAMES
Tropical beaked whale, dense-beaked whale, Atlantic beaked whale.

MAXIMUM LENGTH
16 feet.

MAXIMUM WEIGHT
1 ton.

FIELD ID
(Male only). Dark upperside, lighter underside; fairly prominent fin two-thirds of the way along back; strongly-arched lower jaw; thick, moderately long beak; huge, hornlike teeth; flattened forehead; many oval scars, some scratching.

DIET
Squid and octopuses.

BREEDING
Calving interval and gestation period unknown.

Blainville's beaked whale has a wider distribution than almost any other known beaked whale, but sightings are still relatively rare. Most of our knowledge comes from dead animals washed ashore—it often strands on oceanic islands on both sides of the equator—and from observations on live animals in just three key hotspots. However, it was one of the first beaked whales to be identified when, in 1817, Henri de Blainville managed to describe it from a small piece of jaw. His specimen was the heaviest bone structure he had ever seen (denser even than elephant ivory) and this gave rise to its other common name, the dense-beaked whale. The male has a distinctive, high-arched jawline, with two large teeth on the crest that grow forward and protrude from both sides of the closed mouth. The teeth are not always

female

visible, though, as they can be obscured by stalked barnacles. Blainville's beaked whales make deep dives for food that can last for up to 45 minutes.

Where to look

It is mainly found in tropical to warm temperate waters worldwide, especially in deep water and around gullies on the continental slope. Occasional records in higher latitudes may be linked to warm water currents. There are only three areas where Blainville's beaked whale is observed on a regular basis: the northeastern Bahamas; Oahu, Hawaii; and Moorea in the Society Islands of the South Pacific.

male

Perrin's Beaked Whale
Mesoplodon perrini

ID FACT FILE

OTHER NAMES
None.
MAXIMUM LENGTH
14 feet.
MAXIMUM WEIGHT
Unknown.
FIELD ID
(Male only). Dark
gray above, pale
underneath;
relatively small
size; spindle-
shaped body;
some scarring;
small bulge at
melon; relatively
short beak pale
gray or white;
triangular teeth
near tip of lower
jaw; small dorsal
fin.
DIET
Probably squid
and some fish.
BREEDING
Calving interval
and gestation
period unknown.

Perrin's beaked whale is the most recent
addition to the cetacean list, and was
described as a new species with the
current scientific name in 2002. It is
known from just five animals, which
stranded along the coast of California
between 1975 and 1997. There was
considerable confusion over identification
at first and four were initially identified as
Hector's beaked whales and the fifth as
Cuvier's beaked whale. However, detailed
genetic studies revealed that they
belonged to a new species. It now seems
likely that sightings of two small beaked
whales off California in 1976 and 1978,
which were identified as Hector's beaked
whales, are more likely to have been
Perrin's. There are subtle differences
between the two species. Perrin's beaked
whale was named after W. F. Perrin, who
collected two of the known specimens.

male

Where to look
Known only from five strandings in California, between
Torrey Pines State Reserve just north of San Diego and
Fisherman's Wharf in Monterey, this suggests a range in the
eastern North Pacific. However, this is very limited evidence
and it is possible that the true distribution is much broader.
Like other beaked whales, it is likely to be found in oceanic
waters deeper than 3,300 feet.

Hector's Beaked Whale
Mesoplodon hectori

Until recently, information about Hector's beaked whale was confusing. It was known mostly from stranded animals in two widely separated parts of the world: in the southern hemisphere and many thousands of miles away along the coast of California. But the four animals stranded in California between 1975 and 1997 (originally identified as Hector's beaked whales) are now known to be a recently described species, Perrin's

male

beaked whale. Hector's beaked whale has never been reliably identified alive in the wild. Little is known about its abundance, but it is considered to be one of the rarer beaked whales. Like Hector's dolphin, this species was named after Sir James Hector, the curator of the colonial museum in Wellington, New Zealand.

ID FACT FILE

OTHER NAMES
New Zealand beaked whale, skew-beaked whale.
MAXIMUM LENGTH
14 feet.
MAXIMUM WEIGHT
Unknown.
FIELD ID
(Male only). Dark upperside, lighter underside; small, spindle-shaped body; large, slightly triangular teeth on tip of lower jaw; small, triangular and slightly falcate dorsal fin two-thirds of the way along back.
DIET
Probably squid and some fish.
BREEDING
Calving interval and gestation period unknown.

Where to look
Most records of Hector's beaked whale are from New Zealand, but it seems to have a circumpolar distribution in cool, temperate waters of the southern hemisphere. There are also records from Chile, Argentina, the Falkland Islands, South Africa, and Tasmania. Earlier records of Hector's beaked whales in the northern hemisphere are now known to be Perrin's beaked whale.

Gervais' Beaked Whale

Mesoplodon europaeus

ID FACT FILE

OTHER NAMES
Gulf Stream beaked whale, Antillean beaked whale.

MAXIMUM LENGTH
17 feet.

MAXIMUM WEIGHT
1.5 tons.

FIELD ID
(Male only). Medium-sized, slender body; dark gray upperside, paler gray underside; spindle-shaped body; some linear scarring; fairly long, narrow beak; teeth barely visible one-third of the way back from tip of jaw; small fin two-thirds of the way down back.

DIET
Probably squid and some fish.

BREEDING
Calving interval and gestation period unknown.

Gervais' beaked whale is another poorly known member of the family that has never been reliably identified alive at sea. Consequently, nearly everything we know about its distribution, abundance, and natural history has been gleaned from a relatively small number of strandings. The type specimen (used to describe the species) was found floating dead in the English Channel in 1840— hence it was scientifically named *Mesoplodon europaeus* in 1855 and, for a while at least, dubbed the European beaked whale. However, most records are from warmer waters farther south, along the Atlantic coast of North America, in the

Caribbean, and in the Gulf of Mexico. Intriguingly, a count of tooth layers in one particular stranded individual suggests that it was at least 27 years old.

Where to look
This whale is found in deep tropical and warm temperate waters in the western North Atlantic, with scattered records in the eastern North Atlantic: western Africa, the Canary Islands, and Ireland. It is also known from Ascension Island, in the South Atlantic. There is no information on its abundance, although it does strand along the Atlantic coast of North America (especially in Florida) more than any other *Mesoplodon* species.

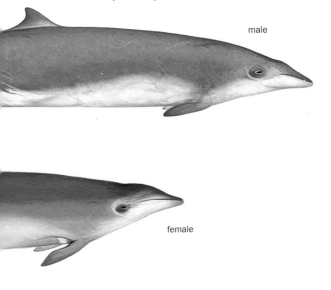

male

female

Ginkgo-toothed Beaked Whale

Mesoplodon ginkgodens

ID FACT FILE

OTHER NAMES
Ginkgo beaked
whale, Japanese
beaked whale.

MAXIMUM LENGTH
16 feet.

MAXIMUM WEIGHT
Unknown.

FIELD ID
(Male only)
Relatively small,
robust body; dark
upperside,
possibly lighter
underside; little
or no linear
scarring; white
spots and
blotches;
smoothly-sloping
forehead; arched
lower jaw; teeth
barely visible on
arch; small fin
two-thirds of the
way along back.

DIET
Probably
squid
and
some fish.

BREEDING
Calving interval
and gestation
period unknown.

The ginkgo-toothed beaked whale is
named for the male's strangely flattened
teeth, which are shaped like the leaves of
a ginkgo tree. This is a common tree in
Japan, where the first specimen of this
whale was found and described in 1958.
These teeth are about 4 inches wide,
making them the widest of any known
Mesoplodon species. The ginkgo-toothed
beaked whale has never been identified
alive at sea and is very poorly known.
Most information comes from stranded
animals found on shore and a handful of
individuals killed by Japanese whalers.
Unlike many of its relatives, the male has
very few (if any) linear scars
on its body. This suggests
that males do not
fight over

dominance hierarchies or females. However, males do have white spots and blotches, especially around the navel, which may be parasitic scars rather than true pigmentation.

Where to look

This species is known only from a small number of widely scattered records in the tropical and warm temperate waters of the Pacific and Indian oceans, from Japan and California to the Galapagos Islands and the Maldives. The ginkgo-toothed beaked whale was being hunted on an opportunistic basis by shore-based whalers in Japan and Taiwan even before it had been scientifically described. There is no information on abundance.

male

Gray's Beaked Whale

Mesoplodon grayi

ID FACT FILE

OTHER NAMES
Haast's beaked
whale,
scamperdown
whale, southern
beaked whale,
small-toothed
beaked whale.

MAXIMUM LENGTH
18 feet.

MAXIMUM WEIGHT
1.3 tons.

FIELD ID
(Male only).
Slender, spindle-
shaped body;
dark upperside,
lighter underside;
very long,
slender,
predominantly
white beak;
slightly bulging
melon; small,
triangular teeth
visible about
one-third of way
back from tip of
beak; small,
falcate fin two-
thirds of the way
along back.

DIET
Probably squid
and some fish.

BREEDING
Calving interval
and gestation
period unknown.

Gray's beaked whales are among the
better known *Mesoplodon* species.
Named in 1876 after John Edward Gray,
a zoologist at the British Museum, they
seem to be more active at the surface
than other beaked whales and are among
the few that have been photographed
alive at sea. This species is unique in the
Mesoplodon genus because adults of both
sexes have 34–44 tiny, evenly spaced
teeth in the upper jaw. Adult males also
have two teeth on the lower jaw. Like the
other beaked whales with especially long
beaks, they often lift their beaks out of
the water at an angle of about 45 degrees
when surfacing. Although
normally encountered
or stranded

in small groups of up to eight animals, in 1874 there was a mass stranding of 28 in the Chatham Islands, east of New Zealand. This species is believed to be one of the most gregarious members of the family.

Where to look

Gray's beaked whale has a circumpolar distribution in temperate waters of the southern hemisphere, mainly in the Southern Ocean south of 30°S. There is a single record from the northern hemisphere—a stranding in the Netherlands in 1927—but this is believed to have been exceptional and well outside the normal range. The high number of strandings suggests that it is fairly common and widespread.

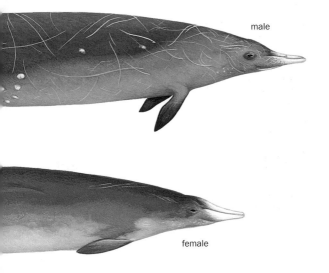

male

female

Strap-toothed Whale

Mesoplodon layardii

ID FACT FILE

OTHER NAMES
Layard's beaked
whale.
MAXIMUM LENGTH
20 feet.
MAXIMUM WEIGHT
1.5 tons.
FIELD ID
(Male only).
Strong dark and
light markings;
considerable
body scarring;
small fin two-
thirds of the way
along back; teeth
curled around
upper jaw; long,
slender beak;
slightly bulging
melon; dark face
"mask"; beak
may break
surface first;
difficult to
approach.
DIET
Squid.
BREEDING
Calving interval
and gestation
period unknown.

The male strap-toothed whale is the
largest member of the *Mesoplodon*
genus. It has two extraordinary teeth,
which grow from its lower jaw, curl
upward and backward, and then extend
over the top of its upper jaw. In older
animals, they sometimes meet in the
middle, forming a muzzle and
preventing the whale from opening its
jaws more than a very few inches. The
teeth may act as "guard rails," helping
the whale to catch squid, its main prey,
while it uses its mouth to suck like a
vacuum cleaner. But this would not
explain why such "wraparound" teeth
are absent in females. A more likely
explanation is that the teeth are a sexual
characteristic, perhaps used in fighting

or in some other way to determine the fittest
males for mating. The variety of tooth formations
originally led to the naming of at least four new
species, but scientists now recognize that they are
in fact all the same species. The strap-toothed
whale was described by John Edward Gray, in
1865, from drawings sent by a curator of the
South African Museum called E. L. Layard—
thus its alternative name.

Where to look
The strap-toothed whale has a wide distribution in
cool temperate waters of the southern hemisphere,
roughly between 30°S and the Antarctic
Convergence. It has stranded on beaches in Chile,
Argentina, Uruguay, the Falkland Islands, southern
Africa, New Zealand, and Australia. Although
poorly known, it appears to be relatively common.

male

True's Beaked Whale

Mesoplodon mirus

ID FACT FILE

OTHER NAMES
Wonderful
beaked whale.
MAXIMUM LENGTH
17 feet.
MAXIMUM WEIGHT
1.4 tons.
FIELD ID
(Male only).
Rotund body;
dark upperside,
light underside
(white tail, fin,
and flukes in
southern
hemisphere);
slightly bulbous
melon; medium-
sized beak; small
teeth at tip of
lower jaw; dark
patch around
eye; linear
scarring; fin two-
thirds of the way
along back.
DIET
Probably squid
and some fish.
BREEDING
Calving interval
and gestation
period unknown.

The distribution of True's beaked whale
has puzzled scientists for some time. It
has two widely separate populations, in
the North Atlantic and the southern
Indian Ocean, and there have been no
sightings or strandings in the huge gap in
between. The two populations are also
quite different in appearance. The
southern hemisphere form has an all-
white tail stock, dorsal fin, and flukes,
which is absent in the North Atlantic
form. But it is still unclear
whether
these are
separate
subspecies or
even species. There have
been a few reliable sightings of True's
beaked whales at sea, most notably, a
group of three whales (believed to be two
adult females and a large calf) off
Hatteras Inlet, North Carolina. In July
2001, a single male was observed
breaching 24 times 31 miles
north of the
Spanish
coast in the
southern
Bay of Biscay. The
species was described in 1913
by American biologist Frederick
W. True, who named it *mirus*
(meaning "wonderful").

Where to look

There are two apparently separate populations
of True's beaked whale. One lives in the warm
temperate waters of the North Atlantic (strandings
have been recorded mainly along the east coast of
the United States and Canada, but also in Ireland,
France, Spain, the Canary Islands, and the Azores).
The other is in the southern Indian Ocean, with
strandings in South Africa and Australia.

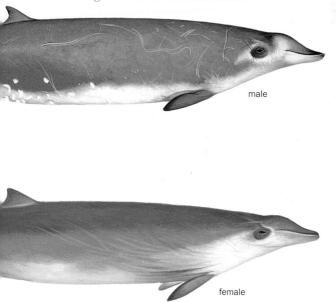

male

female

Stejneger's Beaked Whale

Mesoplodon stejnegeri

ID FACT FILE

OTHER NAMES
Bering Sea
beaked whale,
North Pacific
beaked whale,
saber-toothed
whale.

MAXIMUM LENGTH
17 feet.

MAXIMUM WEIGHT
Possibly 1.5 tons.

FIELD ID
(Male only).
Spindle-shaped,
predominantly
dark body;
extensive linear
scarring;
dark, gently
sloping forehead;
may be lighter
around face;
strongly arched
mouthline; large,
tusklike teeth on
front of arch;
small, falcate fin
two-thirds of the
way along back.

DIET
Squid and
possibly some
fish.

BREEDING
Calving interval
and gestation
period unknown.

For nearly a century, the only evidence for the existence of Stejneger's beaked whale came from a single skull found on Bering Island, in the mid-nineteenth century. But since the late 1970s information about this enigmatic whale has improved and there are now more specimens available for study. In particular, in 1994 a group of four adult females stranded in the Aleutian Islands—

male

providing the first Stejneger's beaked whales in good condition. The male has extraordinary tusklike teeth, second only in size to the teeth of strap-toothed whales, which are set about 8 inches from the tip of the jaw immediately in front of the apex. They are laterally compressed and tilt forward, sometimes converging toward one another and cutting into the upper lip. The species was named in 1855 after the man who found the first skull, Leonhard Stejneger.

Where to look
Cool temperate and subarctic waters of the North
Pacific (from California to Japan) and in the
southwestern Bering Sea. Stejneger's may also range
into warm temperate waters, but the only evidence
for this is the presence of scars inflicted by cookie-
cutter sharks (the sharks are more abundant in
warmer waters further south).

The Aleutian Islands may be a key center of
distribution and there appears to be a distinct
population in the Sea of Japan.

Pygmy Beaked Whale

Mesoplodon peruvianus

ID FACT FILE

OTHER NAMES
Peruvian beaked whale, lesser beaked whale.

MAXIMUM LENGTH
13 feet.

MAXIMUM WEIGHT
Unknown.

FIELD ID
(Male only).
Small size; spindle-shaped body; dark upperside, lighter underside; linear scarring; slightly bulbous melon; slightly sloping forehead; small beak with slightly arched jaw; teeth just visible in front of arch; small, triangular fin two-thirds of the way along back.

DIET
Fish and probably squid.

BREEDING
Calving interval and gestation period unknown.

The pygmy beaked whale is the smallest member of the family and one of the most recent cetacean species to be named. Scientists first became aware of its existence in 1976, when a skull was discovered at a fish market near San Andrés, in Peru. The first complete specimen (a female) was found in 1985, at another fish market just south of Lima, in Peru, and the first adult male was found three years later. In 1990, there were two strandings in La Paz Bay, Baja California, Mexico—the first outside Peruvian waters. The new species was officially named in 1991. Since then, it has been reliably identified at sea on several occasions, but almost nothing is known about its social structure or behavior. There is also no information on abundance, but because many of the first specimens had been caught by fishermen off the coast of Peru, it raises alarm bells about what appears to be a high level of incidental catch.

Where to look

Limited records suggest they are found in mid- to deep waters in the eastern tropical and temperate Pacific, mainly off the coasts of Peru and Chile, but extending from northern Mexico or southern California to northern Chile. However, the range may be more extensive because there is also a possible record—a stranding—from New Zealand.

female

male

Spade-Tooted Whale
Mesoplodon traversii

ID FACT FILE

OTHER NAMES
Bahamonde's
beaked whale.

MAXIMUM LENGTH
Possibly 18 feet
(based on skull
size).

MAXIMUM WEIGHT
Unknown.

FIELD ID
Similarities
in skull
characteristics
suggest that it
may be closely
related to
Andrews' beaked
whale and,
consequently, may
be similar in
appearance.

DIET
Probably squid
and fish.

BREEDING
Calving interval
and gestation
period unknown.

Part of a strange skull, belonging to an immature beaked whale, was found on Robinson Crusoe Island, in the Juan Fernández islands off Chile, in June 1986. After nearly a decade of painstaking examination by some of the world's leading beaked whale experts, it was officially named in 1995 as a species new to science. Since then, it has been discovered that two more specimens (part of a skull from New Zealand and an old tooth and jaw from the Chatham Islands) are genetically identical to the Chilean skull. It is possible that Spade-toothed whale and the so-called "unidentified beaked whale," known only from sightings in the Eastern Tropical Pacific, belong to the same species—but until complete specimens are found this is merely conjecture.

The scientific name has recently been changed from *Mesoplodon bahamondi*.

Spade-toothed whale
skull

Where to look

Currently known only from the Juan Fernández Archipelago, some 366 miles to the west of mainland Chile, and New Zealand (including the Chatham Islands). This would suggest a range across the South Pacific, but there is far too little evidence to be certain.

Shepherd's Beaked Whale

Tasmacetus shepherdi

Shepherd's beaked whale is the only member of the family with a full set of functional teeth in both jaws (Gray's beaked whale has tiny, vestigial teeth in the upper jaw). These occur in both sexes, though only the male has a pair of enlarged teeth at the tip of the lower jaw as in other beaked whales. Since most records are based on partly decomposed animals washed ashore, there is little information on its appearance.

male

Shepherd's beaked whale was described by W. B. B. Oliver in 1937 from a nearly complete skeleton collected by a curator at the Wanganui Alexander Museum in New Zealand, G. Shepherd.

Where to look

Shepherd's beaked whales are known from strandings in New Zealand, the Chatham Islands, Australia, Argentina, the Juan Fernández Islands off Chile, Tristan da Cunha, and the South Sandwich Islands. More than half of these were in New Zealand. Assuming that a sighting in the Seychelles was exceptional, this limited evidence suggests that it may be circumpolar in cool temperate waters between 33°S and 50°S.

ID FACT FILE

OTHER NAMES
Tasman beaked whale, Tasman whale.

MAXIMUM LENGTH
23 feet.

MAXIMUM WEIGHT
Unknown.

FIELD ID
(Male only). Moderately large, spindle-shaped body; dark upperside, light patches on sides, underside and tail stock; light patch on bulbous melon; long, narrow, pointed beak with small teeth on tip; small, slightly falcate fin two-thirds of the way along back.

DIET
Probably squid and fish in equal quantities.

BREEDING
Calving interval and gestation period unknown.

Tropical Bottlenose Whale

Indopacetus pacificus

ID FACT FILE

OTHER NAMES
Pacific beaked whale, Indo-Pacific beaked whale, Longman's beaked whale

MAXIMUM LENGTH
Possibly 26 feet (Maldivian female 19 feet).

MAXIMUM WEIGHT
Unknown.

FIELD ID
(Male only). Relatively large size; brownish upperside, lighter underside; bulbous melon; visible low, bushy blow; moderately long, stubby beak; two teeth near tip of lower jaw (presumably erupting in male only); falcate fin two-thirds of the way along back.

DIET
Probably squid and fish.

BREEDING
Calving interval and gestation period unknown.

Until recently, tropical bottlenose whales were one of the least known cetaceans. The only evidence for its existence came from two weathered skulls. One was discovered in 1882 on a beach near MacKay, in Queensland, Australia, and the other in 1955 on the floor of a fertilizer factory in Mogadishu, Somalia (later traced to a beach near Danane, where it had been picked up by a local fisherman). But in recent years four new specimens have been found, including two juvenile males stranded on the Indian Ocean coast of South Africa, an adult female stranded in the Maldives, and a skull found in Kenya. Sadly, there is still no adult male available for study. However, in the past couple of years there have been some reliable sightings of tropical bottlenose whales at sea (especially in the Maldives). In addition, large beaked whales occasionally reported from the warmer waters of the Indian and Pacific Oceans—are now believed to have been tropical bottlenose whales. The species was named by Heber Longman, a curator at the Queensland Museum, Australia, who recognized the 1882 skull as belonging to a new species.

Where to look

Based on limited evidence from just six specimens and a small number of reliable sightings at sea, tropical bottlenose whales appear to be distributed in the western reaches of the tropical Pacific Ocean and in the western, northern, and southern tropical Indian Ocean. Tropical bottlenose whales have been reported throughout the tropical Indo-Pacific.

Cuvier's Beaked Whale

Ziphius cavirostris

ID FACT FILE

OTHER NAMES
Goose-beaked whale.
MAXIMUM LENGTH
23 feet.
MAXIMUM WEIGHT
3 tons.
FIELD ID
(Male only).
Rotund body;
small head
shaped like
goose's beak;
white head;
small teeth at tip
of jaw; small,
falcate fin set
about two-thirds
along back; low,
inconspicuous
blow; long and
circular scars;
usually alone or
in small groups.
DIET
Mainly squid, but
sometimes fish
and possibly
crustaceans.
BREEDING
Calving interval
and gestation
period unknown.

When Cuvier's beaked whale was first described by the French anatomist Georges Cuvier, in 1823, it was believed to be extinct. However, it is now known to be one of the most abundant and widespread of the beaked whales and is one of the three most watched members of the family (along with Baird's beaked whale and the northern bottlenose whale). The shape of its head and beak is sometimes described as resembling a goose's beak, which explains its alternative name, the goose-beaked whale. Cuvier's beaked whales vary enormously in color, but are among the few ziphiids that can be readily identified at sea. Older males, in particular, are often heavily scarred from the teeth of other males and from bites by cookie-cutter sharks. The two teeth erupt only in males and can be

male

female

seen protruding from the tip of the lower jaw, even
when the mouth is closed; they sometimes have
stalked barnacles growing on them. Cuvier's beaked
whales strand more than any other member of the
beaked whale family.

Where to look

Widely distributed from the tropics to cool
temperate waters worldwide, Cuvier's beaked
whales seem to have very specific habitat
requirements—deep waters on the steepest portion
of the continental slope. It is difficult to predict
sightings, but a few of the hotspots where they
are sometimes seen on whale-watching trips include
the Bay of Biscay, the Canary Islands, the
Mediterranean, and Hawaii.

Baird's Beaked Whale

Berardius bairdii

ID FACT FILE

OTHER NAMES
Giant bottlenose whale, four-toothed whale.

MAXIMUM LENGTH
42 feet.

MAXIMUM WEIGHT
12 tons.

FIELD ID
Large size; long, dark gray, spindle-shaped body; extensive scarring on older animals; small fin two-thirds of the way along back; prominent, bulbous forehead sloping to long beak; anterior teeth may appear white in bright sunlight; tightly packed groups.

DIET
Squid and fish.

BREEDING
Calves every 3 years or more; gestation possibly as long as 17 months.

The largest member of the family, Baird's beaked whale is very similar to Arnoux's beaked whale. These two species are unusual in having four teeth that erupt in both males and females: one large pair at the tip of the protruding lower jaw and a smaller pair just behind them. Baird's beaked whale was discovered in 1882 when researcher Leonhard Stejneger picked up a four-toothed skull on Bering Island. He published his discovery the following year and named the new species after his colleague, Spencer Baird, who had just been appointed Secretary of the Smithsonian Institution. Like other members of the family, Baird's beaked whales are deep divers. They can probably hold their breath for an hour or more, but most dives last around half an hour;

they are believed to reach depths of at least 3,300 feet on a regular basis. They are usually shy of vessels and difficult to approach, but can be active at the surface and have been observed spyhopping and breaching. The status of Baird's beaked whales is uncertain, but the world population is possibly in the order of a few tens of thousands.

Where to look

Deep temperate and subarctic waters in the North Pacific, especially around submarine escarpments and seamounts. Baird's beaked whales are rarely found close to shore, unless the continental shelf is exceptionally narrow. They have been hunted by the Japanese for centuries and 50–60 are still killed every year under a government quota system, mainly in the waters off the Boso Peninsula, near Tokyo, and off Hokkaido Island in the north.

Arnoux's Beaked Whale
Berardius arnuxii

ID FACT FILE

OTHER NAMES
Southern beaked whale, four-toothed whale, giant bottlenose whale, New Zealand beaked whale.

MAXIMUM LENGTH
32 feet.

MAXIMUM WEIGHT
Unknown.

FIELD ID
Large size; long, dark gray, spindle-shaped body; extensive linear scarring on older animals; bulbous melon; long, dolphinlike beak; teeth at tip of lower jaw may appear white in bright sunlight; small fin two-thirds of the way along back.

DIET
Squid and fish.

BREEDING
May calve every 3 years; gestation possibly as long as 17 months.

Arnoux's beaked whale is a very poorly known whale, resembling Baird's beaked whale so closely that for many years it was uncertain whether Baird's represented a geographically isolated form of Arnoux's. But recent genetic studies seem to have settled the dispute in favor of two separate species. The main visible difference appears to be in size. Arnoux's is slightly smaller than Baird's. The two beaked whales would probably be indistinguishable at sea, although their ranges do not appear to overlap and it is highly unlikely that they would ever come into contact with one another. They are among the least sexually dimorphic members of the family—both males and females have erupted teeth and look remarkably similar. Named after a French surgeon, M. Arnoux, who presented the first skull to the Paris Museum of Natural History in 1846, Arnoux's beaked whale is usually shy and difficult to observe.

Where to look

Arnoux's beaked whales appear to inhabit vast areas of the southern hemisphere, from the Antarctic to southern Brazil, South Georgia, South Africa, New Zealand, and Australia. Most records show them to be south of 40°S from temperate to Antarctic waters. They are not known in the tropics. There is no information on abundance but, unlike its northern hemisphere relative, Arnoux's beaked whale is not taken by commercial whalers.

Northern Bottlenose Whale

Hyperoodon ampullatus

ID FACT FILE

OTHER NAMES
North Atlantic bottlenosed whale, flathead, bottlehead, steephead.

MAXIMUM LENGTH
32 feet.

MAXIMUM WEIGHT
7.5 tons.

One of the three most watched members of the family (along with Cuvier's beaked whale and Baird's beaked whale), the northern bottlenose whale is a curious animal and frequently approaches stationary or slow-moving boats. Its most distinctive feature is its huge bulbous

FIELD ID
(Male only). Long, robust, cylindrical body; dark, yellow-brown upperside, lighter underside; bulbous melon often pale and squared off; prominent beak; teeth at tip rarely visible; falcate fin; visible, bushy blow; may be curious.

DIET
Mainly squid, some fish, crustaceans, and invertebrates.

BREEDING Calves every 2–3 years; gestation about 12 months.

forehead, which is most prominent in older males. There are two teeth at the tip of the lower jaw (erupting in males only) and these are sometimes covered in stalked barnacles. Capable of diving to depths of 5,000 feet, it can remain submerged for over an hour. Hunted more than any other beaked whale, it has now been protected for more than a quarter of a century.

Where to look

The northern bottlenose whale lives in the North Atlantic, mainly north of the Iberian Peninsula in the east and Nova Scotia in the west. It prefers deep water. Little is known about its seasonal movements. It appears to be present all year in the Gully (a submarine canyon off Nova Scotia) but only in summer in the southern Bay of Biscay.

Southern Bottlenose Whale

Hyperoodon planifrons

The southern bottlenose whale is very poorly known. It lives far from shipping lanes, and has never been heavily exploited, so most information comes from strandings and incidental observations by researchers. It is not difficult to identify at sea, though it does look similar to Arnoux's beaked whale from a distance and the two species have almost identical ranges. The chocolatey yellow-brown color is believed to be caused by a thin layer of diatoms (single-celled algae) as well as by natural pigmentation. Southern bottlenose whales are usually found in small groups (one to four individuals is typical), although up to 20 have been observed together. Approximate abundance estimates for the region south of the Antarctic Convergence in summer suggest a population of half a million.

ID FACT FILE

OTHER NAMES
Antarctic bottlenosed whale, flathead.

MAXIMUM LENGTH
25 feet.

MAXIMUM WEIGHT
Unknown.

FIELD ID (Male only): Long, robust body; dark, yellow-brown upperside, light underside; can appear almost white at sea; bulbous melon often pale and squared-off; stubby beak; tiny teeth at tip; visible, bushy blow; prominent, falcate fin.

DIET
Squid, some fish and benthic invertebrates.

BREEDING
Possibly calves every 2–3 years; gestation may be about 12 months.

Where to look

Found throughout the cold, deep waters of the southern hemisphere, from the Antarctic ice edge to about 30ºS (with occasional sightings farther north), limited evidence suggests that there are seasonal movements in some populations. The highest density, for instance, occurs during summer within about 60 miles of the Antarctic ice edge.

Pygmy Killer Whale
Feresa attenuata

ID FACT FILE

OTHER NAMES
Lesser killer
whale, slender
blackfish,
slender pilot
whale.

MAXIMUM LENGTH
8 feet 6 inches.

MAXIMUM WEIGHT
375 pounds.

FIELD ID
Robust, dark-
colored body;
slightly paler gray
sides, white
patch on
underside; dark
dorsal cape
visible in some
light conditions;
rounded head
with no beak and
white lips; some
individuals have
white chin;
prominent
falcate fin.

DIET
Mostly fish and
squid.

BREEDING
Calving interval
and gestation
period unknown.

Although no bigger than a dolphin itself,
the pygmy killer whale is known to attack
other small cetaceans in the wild and has
been quite aggressive toward other
species and even people in captivity.
Although it is widely distributed, it is not
particularly well known. There are
reports of bow-riding and wake-riding,
but it tends to be less active than most
oceanic dolphins and usually avoids
boats. Schools often swim abreast in long
"chorus lines" and, when alarmed, bunch
together—often leaping clear of the
water in their determination to rush
away. When viewed at close range, it is
possible to see a distinctive white chin on
some individuals and the white lips that
are common in this species. It is similar
in size to many oceanic dolphins, though
is most likely to be confused with the

similar-looking melon-headed whale. Generally speaking, if a small number of animals are seen together (fewer than 50) they are more likely to be pygmy killer whales.

Where to look

Found worldwide in deep, offshore waters mainly in the tropics and subtropics but also in warm temperate regions, the pygmy killer whale rarely occurs close to shore except around oceanic islands. Small numbers are drowned in fishing nets and caught up in drive fisheries in Japan, Sri Lanka, and elsewhere, and in several countries (especially in Asia) they are harpooned opportunistically.

Melon-headed Whale

Peponocephala electra

ID FACT FILE

OTHER NAMES
Little killer whale, electra dolphin, many-toothed blackfish.
MAXIMUM LENGTH
9 feet.
MAXIMUM WEIGHT
463 pounds.
FIELD ID
Small, torpedo-shaped body; overall dark gray or black color, some white on underside; dark dorsal cape and facial markings visible in certain lights; slim, pointed head (from above); little or no beak; white, light gray, or pink lips; large, falcate fin.
DIET
Mostly fish and squid, some crustaceans.
BREEDING
Calving interval unknown; gestation possibly about 12 months.

There seems to have been some confusion over the melon-headed whale's common name. The scientific word *Peponocephala* was believed to mean "melon-headed"—"pepo" was thought to be Latin for "melon"—and so was used to describe the distinctively-shaped, pointed head of this species. But another definition of pepo in Latin is a "pumpkin." So, one might also refer to the melon-headed whale as a pumpkin-headed whale. Despite its wide distribution, it is infrequently encountered at sea except at certain hotspots such as the Maldives, Cebu Island in the Philippines, Hawaii, and off the east coast of Australia. It often creates a lot of spray as it surfaces, and frequently changes direction underwater, making it difficult to see in any detail. Confusion is most likely with the pygmy killer whale, which is very similar in appearance. Generally speaking, if there are several hundred animals together they are more likely to be melon-headed whales. Also, unlike pygmy killer whales, they are sometimes encountered in mixed schools with Fraser's dolphins.

Where to look

Mainly found in deep, subtropical, and tropical waters worldwide, the melon-headed whale is most common between about 20°N and 20°S. It is sometimes observed in temperate regions, though these are probably strays traveling in warm currents. Melon-headed whales are usually encountered offshore, and rarely venture close to shore except around oceanic islands or where the water is deep. Some drown in fishing nets and they are harpooned throughout their range.

False Killer Whale

Pseudorca crassidens

ID FACT FILE

OTHER NAMES
False pilot whale, pseudorca.

MAXIMUM LENGTH
20 feet.

MAXIMUM WEIGHT
2 tons.

FIELD ID
Relatively long and slender body; uniformly dark except for light areas on throat and chest; slender, rounded or conical head with no beak; melon overhangs tip of lower jaw (adult male only); unique "elbow" on flippers; prominent, falcate fin; fairly acrobatic.

DIET
Mostly fish and squid, known to attack other cetaceans.

BREEDING
Calving interval possibly up to 7 years; gestation 14–16 months.

The false killer whale can look rather menacing and has been known to attack groups of small cetaceans. On one occasion it even attacked a nursery school of sperm whales and, on another, killed a humpback whale calf. Yet it is often seen in the company of bottlenose dolphins and, in captivity, shows less aggression than its smaller relative the pygmy killer whale. One of the largest members of the dolphin family, in many ways it behaves more like an oceanic dolphin: it leaps high into the air, makes rapid turns underwater, and even rides the bow-waves of boats and ships. It is a fast and active swimmer, often lifting its entire head and much of its body out of the water when it surfaces. False killer whales seem to be susceptible to stranding, and sometimes come ashore in huge numbers (more than 800 in one exceptional case). They normally occur in groups of around 20 animals, but it is not unusual for many smaller groups to travel together. They are unpopular with fishermen and have a reputation for

stealing fish such as tuna from baited lines. The
common name refers to a similarity in skull
morphology with the killer whale, rather than a
similarity in external appearance.

Where to look

Widely distributed in tropical, subtropical, and
warm temperate waters worldwide (including
enclosed seas such as the Mediterranean and Red
Sea). False killer whales prefer deep water and,
except around oceanic islands, are normally
encountered offshore. Small numbers drown in
fishing nets and are hunted for food or by fishermen
who regard them as competitors. A few are also
captured for marine parks.

Long-finned Pilot Whale

Globicephala melas

ID FACT FILE

OTHER NAMES
Caaing whale, blackfish, pothead whale.

MAXIMUM LENGTH
21 feet (male), 16 feet (female).

MAXIMUM WEIGHT
Possibly 3 tons.

FIELD ID
Long, stocky body; black, gray or dark brown; pale saddle-patch behind fin; large, rounded head with bulbous melon; light diagonal stripe behind each eye (mainly southern hemisphere); no visible beak; exceptionally long flippers; low, broad-based fin far forward on body (sweeps backward).

DIET
Mainly squid and fish, some crustaceans.

BREEDING
Calves every 3–5 years; gestation 12 months.

Long-finned and short-finned pilot whales are almost impossible to tell apart at sea but, fortunately, there is relatively little overlap in their range. The main differences are subtle: in the length of the flippers (proportionally longer in long-finned); the shape of the skull (slightly longer and narrower in long-finned); and the number of teeth (a few more in long-finned). There are also significant differences between the vocalizations of the two species. The calls of long-finned pilot whales are of a lower frequency and a narrower frequency range than those of short-finned pilot whales. There are two recognized subspecies of long-finned pilot whale. One is in the northern hemisphere and the other is thousands of miles away in the southern hemisphere. They strand more frequently than many other species and are often involved in mass strandings involving hundreds of animals. Limited estimates of abundance suggest a population of about three-quarters of a million in the central and eastern North Atlantic, at least 10,000 in the western North Atlantic, and some 200,000 in the Southern Ocean.

Where to look
The long-finned pilot whale has two distinct populations. One is in the cool, deep temperate waters of the North Atlantic (including the western Mediterranean Sea) and the other is found throughout the Southern Ocean. These two populations are completely isolated. There is some overlap in range with the short-finned pilot whale. More than 1,000 long-finned pilot whales are killed every year in the Faroe Islands, and smaller numbers in other parts of the world.

Short-finned Pilot Whale

Globicephala macrorhynchus

ID FACT FILE

OTHER NAMES
Pacific pilot whale, blackfish, pothead whale.

MAXIMUM LENGTH
24 feet (male), 17 feet (female).

MAXIMUM WEIGHT
Possibly 4 tons.

FIELD ID
Long, stocky body; black, gray or dark brown; pale saddle-patch behind fin (variable); large, rounded head with bulbous melon; may be light diagonal stripe behind each eye; no visible beak; shorter flippers than long-finned; low, broad-based fin far forward on body (sweeps backward).

DIET
Mainly squid, some fish and octopuses.

BREEDING
Calves every 5–8 years; gestation 15–16 months.

Pilot whales are among the largest members of the dolphin family. Their name originates from an early theory (probably not true) that a school is piloted or led by one particular leader. Both long-finned and short-finned pilot whales exhibit striking sexual dimorphism in size since males are considerably longer than females and have a more pronounced melon and much larger dorsal fin. They are highly social animals, typically living in small groups (10–20 individuals in long-finned and 15–90 in short-finned), which often come together to form much larger gatherings. As in killer whale pods, these close-knit families stay together for life and most individuals never leave (although males mate with females from other groups to avoid inbreeding). Females continue to ovulate until their late thirties and may still be lactating in their late forties; they probably live well into their sixties. Limited estimates of abundance suggest a population of some 160,000 in the eastern tropical Pacific and 30,000–50,000 in southern Japan. Several hundred short-finned pilot whales are killed annually in Japan and the Caribbean, and they are hunted in Indonesia and Sri Lanka.

Where to look

The short-finned pilot whale prefers warm water
and is found worldwide in the tropics and subtropics
and in warm temperate regions. It is common in the
Canary Islands and occurs around Madeira and the
Azores, but is absent from the Mediterranean.
There is little, but probably some, overlap in range
with the long-finned pilot whale—mainly in
temperate waters of the Atlantic, in the Pacific off
the coast of Peru, Tasmania and the southeast coast
of Australia, and off South Africa.

Killer Whale

Orcinus orca

ID FACT FILE

OTHER NAMES
Orca, blackfish.

MAXIMUM LENGTH
30 feet (male),
25 feet (female).

MAXIMUM WEIGHT
Possibly 9 tons
(heaviest on
record 5.6 tons).

FIELD ID
Large, stocky
body; jet black
and brilliant
white coloration;
white patch
behind each eye;
extremely tall,
black triangular
fin of male
(smaller and
falcate in
females and
calves); gray
saddle-patch
behind fin; large,
paddle-shaped
flippers.

DIET
Extremely varied,
from squid and
fish to birds and
marine mammals
(each pod tends
to specialize).

BREEDING
Calving interval
averages 5
years; gestation
15–18 months.

When Basque whalers saw killer whales feeding on the carcasses of dead whales, they called them "whale killers" and the name stuck. But many people prefer to use the more politically correct name, orca, to avoid any negative connotations. Unfortunately, though, the Latin *orcus* means "belonging to the kingdom of the dead." Killer whales have been studied in the wild for more than 30 years. Several distinct forms are known—dubbed residents, transients, and offshores—which differ significantly in appearance, behavior, group size, and diet. Another form living in the Antarctic has been proposed as a separate species, but this is controversial. Studies on resident whales living in the eastern North Pacific show that the basic social unit is the matrilineal group, which consists of up to four generations (a female, her sons and daughters, and the offspring of her daughters); they are all closely related and usually stay together for life. Several matrilineal groups together form an extended family called a pod; and several pods, which share similar dialects, are called a clan. Most killer whale populations are numbered in the hundreds or low thousands, but there may be 70,000–80,000 in the Antarctic.

male

Where to look

Despite its somewhat patchy distribution, the killer whale is one of the most wide-ranging mammals on Earth. It occurs in all seas and oceans, from the equator to the high Arctic and the Antarctic pack ice and from near the coast to far offshore. However, it generally prefers cooler inshore waters. It is still persecuted by some fishermen and periodically caught for public display in aquaria.

Tucuxi

Sotalia fluviatilis

ID FACT FILE

OTHER NAMES
Estuarine
dolphin.

MAXIMUM LENGTH
7 feet (marine),
5 feet
(freshwater).

MAXIMUM WEIGHT
99 pounds.

FIELD ID
Small, robust
body; gray
upperside, light
underside
(sometimes
appears pink—
especially on the
sides and
underside);
prominent, fairly
slender beak;
slightly rounded
melon; roughly
triangular fin (low
in profile).

DIET
Mainly fish,
some
crustaceans.

BREEDING
Calving interval
unknown;
gestation
probably 10
months.

There are two subspecies of tucuxi (pronounced tookooshee). There is a relatively small subspecies found in lakes and rivers, and a considerably larger one in the sea. The riverine form has been studied in some detail, but less is known about the marine form. Despite its large riverine

population, it is a member of the family Delphinidae and is not closely related to the "true" river dolphins (although, in the Amazon Basin, it is not unusual to see tucuxis feeding in the company of Amazon river dolphins). It is often referred to simply as "Sotalia," which is the first part of its scientific name. At first glance it looks rather like a small bottlenose dolphin—and sometimes behaves like one, too. Tucuxis are fairly active at the surface and can be seen breaching, spyhopping, and splashing. They are not known to bow-ride, but will sometimes play in the wake of passing boats and ships. As well as hunting,

incidental capture in fishing nets, and conflicts with
fisheries, the damming of the Amazon, mangrove
degradation, and coastal pollution
are all threats.

Where to look

The tucuxi is found in warm, shallow coastal waters
of northeastern South America and eastern Central
America (from Nicaragua to Florianópolis in Brazil)
and throughout much of the Amazon River basin.
Coastal populations are most common in estuaries
and large bays, while riverine ones are found as far
as 1,550 miles up the Amazon. They appear to be
fairly common over much of their range.

Spinner Dolphin
Stenella longirostris

ID FACT FILE

OTHER NAMES
Long-snouted
spinner,
longsnout,
rollover, long-
beaked dolphin.

MAXIMUM LENGTH
8 feet.

MAXIMUM WEIGHT
200 pounds.

FIELD ID
Slender body;
three-part color
pattern; long,
narrow beak with
dark tip; upper
jaw gray, lower
jaw often cream;
dark stripe from
eye to flipper;
gently sloping
melon; tall fin can
be slightly falcate
or erect (leans
forward in some
individuals);
performs high,
spinning leaps.

DIET
Fish, squid, and
crustaceans.

BREEDING
Calves every 3
years; gestation
just over 10
months.

One of the most acrobatic of all dolphins,
the spinner was named for its incredibly
high spinning leaps. It can spin around
on its longitudinal axis as many as seven
times before splashing back into the
water. No other cetacean shows so much
variation in appearance from one region
to another and there are currently three
recognized subspecies, differing greatly
in body shape, size, color, and even
behavior. The color pattern in most
regions is basically in three parts, albeit
with considerable regional differences,
consisting of a dark gray cape, light gray
sides, and a white underside. Numbers
were reduced significantly by tuna-
fishing in the eastern tropical Pacific
(which has been responsible for killing
more dolphins in the past 35 years than
any other human activity). Fortunately,
public outrage has forced the authorities
to introduce new rules and regulations,
which include releasing dolphins from
the nets when they are captured, and the
scale of the slaughter has dropped to
thousands (rather than hundreds of

thousands) of deaths a year. However, the population of eastern spinners is still probably less than half its original size.

Where to look

The spinner is found mainly in tropical and subtropical waters worldwide, although it sometimes occurs in warm temperate waters as well. Depending on the subspecies, it can be seen in shallow water close to shore, around oceanic islands, or far out to sea. Many spinners are hunted or drowned in gill nets every year, especially in Australia and Asia. Despite all the threats, it is still fairly common in some parts of its range.

Clymene Dolphin
Stenella clymene

ID FACT FILE

OTHER NAMES
Short-snouted spinner dolphin, Senegal dolphin, helmet dolphin.

MAXIMUM LENGTH
6 feet 6 inches.

MAXIMUM WEIGHT
176 pounds.

FIELD ID
Relatively small, fairly robust body; three-toned color pattern; dark gray or black cape dips below fin; long beak with black tip, lips and "mustache"; pale gray stripe from eye to flipper; dark, slender flippers; prominent, slightly falcate or triangular fin.

DIET
Fish and squid.

BREEDING
Calving interval and gestation period unknown.

For many years the clymene dolphin, or short-snouted spinner dolphin as it is often called, was considered to be one of the many variations of the long-snouted spinner. The two animals sometimes associate with one another and, like the spinner, the clymene has a three-toned coloration, which includes a dark gray cape, lighter gray sides, and a white underside. Some populations even spin longitudinally when breaching, although not as frequently or as elaborately as spinners. It was first recognized in 1966, but the clymene dolphin (pronounced cly-mee-nee) was classified as a separate species in 1981. There is considerable overlap in range between the two species in the Atlantic, and they can be difficult to tell apart at sea. The clymene dolphin is usually seen in groups of up to 50 animals (although several hundred have been observed together). Schools may be segregated by sex, and possibly age, since several mass strandings have consisted almost entirely of females or males. It is a keen bow-rider and will go out of its way to accompany a boat or ship, yet remains one of the least known oceanic dolphins.

Where to look

Found in warm temperate, subtropical, and tropical waters of the Atlantic Ocean, the clymene dolphin occurs mainly in deep waters offshore. It appears to be absent from the Mediterranean, but details of its distribution are lacking. Little is also known about its abundance. Some hunting takes place in the Caribbean and it is caught incidentally in fishing nets in many parts of its range, especially in West Africa.

Striped Dolphin
Stenella coeruleoalba

ID FACT FILE

OTHER NAMES
Streaker,
whitebelly.

MAXIMUM LENGTH
9 feet.

MAXIMUM WEIGHT
350 pounds.

FIELD ID
Fairly robust
body; bluish-gray
upperside, pale
gray sides and
tail stock, white
or pinkish
underside; long,
dark side stripe;
pale shoulder
blaze sweeping
up toward fin;
dark stripe from
eye to flipper;
prominent beak;
dark, prominent
fin.

DIET
Squid and fish
(lanternfish a
favorite in some
areas).

BREEDING
Calves every 4
years; gestation
12–13 months.

Striped dolphins are highly conspicuous animals, seeming to spend an inordinate amount of their time in the air. Their acrobatic repertoire includes high breaches, belly-flops, chin-slaps, back somersaults, tail spins, and upside-down porpoising. They also have a unique behavior, called "roto-tailing," which involves leaping into a high arc and then rapidly rotating the tail before re-entering the water. Their distinctive stripes, and the speed at which they swim, prompted fishermen to call them "streakers." In some parts of the world they readily approach boats, but they are more wary and do not bow-ride in the eastern tropical Pacific where, until quite recently, considerable numbers were killed by the tuna-fishing industry. Known to live to the ripe old age of nearly 60 years, they are fairly well known and several different populations have been studied in detail.

Where to look

Found worldwide, striped dolphins live mainly in
tropical, subtropical, and warm temperate waters—
although they occur as far north as southern
Greenland and Iceland. Despite large numbers
being killed incidentally by a pelagic drift-net
fishery, they are probably the commonest cetaceans
in the Mediterranean Sea. Usually encountered
offshore, they are hunted in some regions of the
world, especially in the Japanese drive fishery.

Pantropical Spotted Dolphin

Stenella attenuata

ID FACT FILE

OTHER NAMES
Spotted dolphin, spotter.

MAXIMUM LENGTH
8 feet 6 inches.

MAXIMUM WEIGHT
265 pounds.

FIELD ID
Slender, elongated body (variable); dark gray cape, lighter underside; most adults heavily spotted; long, narrow beak with white tip and lips; thick, dark stripe from beak to flipper; tall, strongly falcate fin.

DIET
Squid and fish, some crustaceans.

BREEDING
Calves every 2–4 years; gestation 11–12 months.

Tuna-fishing operations in the eastern tropical Pacific killed so many pantropical spotted dolphins in the 1960s, 1970s, and 1980s that the regional population declined by as much as 75 percent. Literally millions of the animals were killed, along with huge numbers of other dolphin species. New laws and release techniques have reduced the level of the slaughter dramatically, but it has still not been stopped altogether. It is still unclear why the dolphins associate with tuna. It might be that it increases foraging efficiency or provides better protection from predators. Adults are usually covered in white spots, which fuse and fade to a medium gray as they get older, but newborn calves are unspotted. However, there is a lot of variation in the appearance of individuals within a population and between populations in different parts of the world. Three subspecies are currently recognized: one living mainly in coastal waters of the eastern Pacific tends to be larger, more spotted, and more robust. Pantropical spotted dolphins spend a lot of time in the air and youngsters can make some impressively high vertical leaps.

Where to look

Found worldwide in tropical and some subtropical waters of the Atlantic, Pacific, and Indian oceans, the pantropical spotted dolphin occurs both inshore and offshore. It is most abundant nearer the equator, but is known as far north as 40°N and as far south as 40°S. Although hunted in many parts of the world and caught incidentally in fishing nets, it is still surprisingly abundant and the world population is estimated to be at least three million.

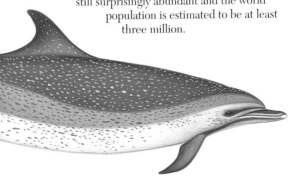

Atlantic Spotted Dolphin
Stenella frontalis

ID FACT FILE

OTHER NAMES
Spotter, bridled dolphin, Gulf Stream spotted dolphin.

MAXIMUM LENGTH
7 feet 6 inches.

MAXIMUM WEIGHT
310 pounds.

FIELD ID
Fairly robust head and body; three-toned color pattern (not always clear); most adults heavily spotted; pale diagonal shoulder blaze sweeping up toward fin; chunky, white-tipped beak; tall, falcate fin; variable appearance within herd.

DIET
Squid and fish, some benthic invertebrates.

BREEDING
Calves every 3–4 years; gestation period unknown.

There are so many variations in the markings of spotted dolphins that their taxonomy has puzzled experts for a long time. But the Atlantic spotted dolphin is one of just two currently recognized species. Most adults have dark spots on the underside and light spots on the sides and back, but some are not spotted at all and others are so heavily spotted they appear almost white from a distance. Young animals have no spots but these begin to appear as they grow older. The Atlantic spotted dolphin is difficult to tell apart from the very similar pantropical spotted dolphin, but the distinctive diagonal shoulder blaze that sweeps up through the cape toward the dorsal fin is diagnostic. One particular population of Atlantic spotted dolphins on Little Bahama Bank, north of the Bahamas, has been studied in great detail since the 1970s, but the species is less well known elsewhere in the Atlantic.

Where to look

As its name suggests, the Atlantic spotted dolphin is found in the Atlantic—both North and South—in warm temperate, subtropical, and tropical waters. The range extends from about 50°N to 25°S, but it does not appear to include the

Mediterranean Sea. Most information is from coastal areas, but sightings are also fairly common far from land. It is hunted in some areas and killed incidentally in fisheries in the Caribbean and West Africa.

Atlantic Hump-backed Dolphin

Sousa teuszii

ID FACT FILE

OTHER NAMES
Cameroon dolphin.

MAXIMUM LENGTH
9 feet.

MAXIMUM WEIGHT
575 pounds.

FIELD ID
Robust body; slate-gray upperside and sides, paler underside; elongated hump on back; small fin sits on hump; long, slender beak; beak exposed on surfacing; back strongly arched on diving; flukes often raised on diving.

DIET
Fish, squid, and octopuses.

BREEDING
Calves every 3 years; gestation 10–12 months.

Once incorrectly believed to be the only plant-eating dolphin, the Atlantic hump-backed dolphin is a strange-looking animal with a conspicuous, elongated hump on its back. The dorsal fin sits on top of the hump, giving it a rather top-heavy appearance. There appears to be no overlap in range with the Indo-Pacific hump-backed dolphin, which just enters the Atlantic at the southern tip of Africa, but recent morphological studies and genetic analyses suggest that it may belong to the same species. Atlantic hump-backed dolphins are well known for joining bottlenose dolphins in cooperating with Mauritanian fishermen around Cap Timiris, north of Nouakchott, by driving fish toward their nets. However, they are threatened throughout their range by entanglement in fishing nets and, in some areas, by hunting. Living very close to shore, in water typically less than 80 feet deep, they are also vulnerable to threats such as habitat destruction and disturbance.

Where to look

There is little information on the precise range of Atlantic hump-backed dolphins, but they are known from the coastal waters of tropical and subtropical West Africa (southern Morocco to Cameroon and possibly as far south as Angola). They certainly appear to have a considerably smaller range than their Indo-Pacific relatives. They are most common around estuaries and mangrove swamps and are known to enter the Niger and some other rivers (though they usually remain within the tidal zone).

Indo-Pacific Hump-backed Dolphin

Sousa chinensis

ID FACT FILE

OTHER NAMES
Chinese white dolphin, pink dolphin.

MAXIMUM LENGTH
9 feet.

MAXIMUM WEIGHT
575 pounds.

FIELD ID
Robust body; gray, brown, pink, white, or mottled color; elongated hump on back (animals west of Sumatra only); small fin sits on hump; long, slender beak; beak exposed on surfacing; back strongly arched on diving; flukes often raised on diving.

DIET
Fish, squid, and octopuses.

BREEDING
Calves every 3 years; gestation 10–12 months.

Indo-Pacific hump-backed dolphins vary greatly in appearance, depending on where they live. The animals west of Sumatra, in Indonesia, have a fatty hump on their backs and a relatively small dorsal fin on top, whereas those living east and south of Sumatra have a less pronounced hump (or no hump at all) but a more prominent dorsal fin. There are also several distinct color variations, including pure white, gray, and even pink. There is an interesting population in the South China Sea, commonly known as Chinese white dolphins, which are white or bright pink in color. Inevitably, the classification of hump-backed dolphins is still under discussion. Some evidence suggests that there should be just one species (*Sousa chinensis*), but other evidence supports the case for three species: Pacific hump-backed (*Sousa chinensis*), Atlantic hump-backed (*Sousa teuszii*), and a third in the Indian Ocean called the Indian hump-backed (*Sousa plumbea*). The hump occurs only in the *teuszii* and *plumbea* forms. They are vulnerable because they live close to the shore and are threatened by hunting in some areas as well as entanglement in fishing nets and antishark nets.

Where to look

Indo-Pacific hump-backed dolphins are found in shallow coastal waters in the tropics and subtropics, from northern Australia and southern China in the east, around the Indian Ocean, to southern Africa in the west. They rarely enter water more than 80 feet deep and are seldom seen more than a few miles from shore. They sometimes enter rivers, though rarely more than a few miles upstream and usually within the tidal zone.

Northern Rightwhale Dolphin

Lissodelphis borealis

ID FACT FILE

OTHER NAMES
Pacific rightwhale porpoise.

MAXIMUM LENGTH
10 feet.

MAXIMUM WEIGHT
250 pounds.

FIELD ID
Streamlined, slender body; predominantly black with white underside; no fin; white spot under short, slender beak; predominantly black flippers; low-angled leaps give impression of bouncy swimming motion.

DIET
Fish (especially lanternfish) and squid.

BREEDING
Calves every 2 years; gestation 12–13 months.

Superficially similar in appearance to its southern counterpart, the northern rightwhale dolphin is the only dolphin in the North Pacific without a dorsal fin. Its striking black-and-white body pattern is also distinctive, though in the water it often appears to be entirely black. The calves of both species are usually dark gray or brown—they become black and white like their parents when they are about a year old. Northern rightwhale

dolphins are capable of swimming very fast, making long, low-angled leaps, and appearing to bounce across the water, but they sometimes surface slowly and keep a low profile. This makes them difficult to see in anything but the calmest conditions. They are often encountered in the company of other cetaceans, especially Pacific white-sided dolphins, and travel in huge schools of up to 3,000 animals. Tens of thousands were killed in the 1980s in drift nets set for squid (which are now banned on the high seas). Relatively small numbers are taken by Japan's harpoon fishery and others are drowned in nets on both sides of the Pacific, especially in the Japanese and Russian purse-seine fisheries.

Where to look
Northern rightwhale dolphins are found in cool temperate and subarctic waters across the northern North Pacific, mainly in deep, offshore waters between 34°N and 55°N (34°N and 47°N in mid-ocean). More southerly records normally occur where the water temperature is unusually low. They are rarely seen near land, except in sufficiently deep water. There is no overlap in range with the southern rightwhale dolphin—the two species are separated by many thousands of miles.

Southern Rightwhale Dolphin

Lissodelphis peronii

ID FACT FILE

OTHER NAMES
Mealy-mouthed porpoise.

MAXIMUM LENGTH
10 feet.

MAXIMUM WEIGHT
265 pounds.

FIELD ID
Streamlined, slender body; stark black-and-white color pattern (jet-black upperside, white underside); no fin; short, white beak; predominantly white flippers; low-angled leaps give impression of bouncy swimming motion.

DIET
Fish (especially lanternfish) and squid.

BREEDING
Calving interval and gestation period unknown.

The only dolphin in the southern hemisphere without a dorsal fin, the southern rightwhale dolphin is very distinctive with its striking black-and-white body pattern. Despite its remote offshore distribution, it is fairly easy to see in the right areas and will sometimes even bow-ride. From a distance, schools of fast-swimming southern rightwhale

dolphins look remarkably similar to penguins; and, when swimming slowly, they can be mistaken for porpoising fur seals or sea lions. Slow swimming gives them a very low profile and makes them difficult to see in anything but the calmest conditions. They travel in large schools of up to 1,000 animals and often associate with long-finned pilot whales or dusky dolphins. They are killed for human consumption or crab bait off Chile and Peru, and increasing numbers drown in fishing nets in the rapidly developing swordfish gill-net fishery off Chile. Both northern and southern rightwhale dolphins were named after the much larger right whales, which also lack dorsal fins.

Where to look

Found mainly between the Tropic of Capricorn and the Antarctic Convergence, southern rightwhale dolphins live in the cold temperate to subantarctic waters of the southern hemisphere. They occur farther north in some parts of their range, especially where cold currents such as the Humboldt and Benguela push into subtropical latitudes. Rarely seen near land, they prefer deep water.

Short-beaked Common Dolphin

Delphinus delphis

ID FACT FILE

OTHER NAMES
Criss-cross
dolphin,
saddleback
dolphin, white-
bellied porpoise,
common
porpoise.

MAXIMUM LENGTH
9 feet.

MAXIMUM WEIGHT
330 pounds.

FIELD ID
Slightly robust
body; criss-cross
pattern on sides;
dark cape with
"V" directly
under fin; yellowy
tan patch on
sides, white
underside, pale
gray tail stock;
dark line from
flipper to beak;
prominent beak;
tall, moderately
falcate fin; crisp
color pattern.

DIET
Fish and squid.

BREEDING
Calves every 1–3
years; gestation
10–11 months.

There are many different forms of common dolphin around the world and numerous species have been proposed over the years. They all have the distinctive hourglass pattern of white, gray, yellow, and black on their sides, but show many differences within this basic framework. In 1995, though, the common dolphin was officially separated into two distinct species, now known as the short-beaked common dolphin and the long-beaked common dolphin. These show many subtle genetic, physical, and behavioral differences, though, at sea, they can still be very difficult to tell apart. In general terms, the short-beaked is a little more robust, with a slightly shorter beak and crisper color pattern. There are also subtle differences in the facial pattern. Huge numbers of short-beaked common dolphins were killed by Turkish and Russian fishermen in the Black Sea, severely depleting the population there by the time hunting ceased in the 1980s. Significant numbers are drowned in fishing nets across their range, and local populations seem to be declining in some areas.

SHORT-BEAKED COMMON DOLPHIN

Where to look

The short-beaked common dolphin is the most
numerous dolphin in offshore warm temperate,
subtropical, and tropical waters of the Atlantic and
Pacific Oceans. It is especially common in deep
water along the shelf edge and over seamounts and
submarine canyons, but sometimes occurs in
shallower water close to shore. It occurs in both the
Mediterranean and Black Seas.

Long-beaked Common Dolphin

Delphinus capensis

ID FACT FILE

OTHER NAMES
Criss-cross
dolphin,
saddleback
dolphin, white-
bellied porpoise,
common
porpoise.

MAXIMUM LENGTH
8 feet.

MAXIMUM WEIGHT
330 pounds.

FIELD ID
Slender body;
criss-cross
pattern on sides;
dark cape with
"V" under fin;
yellow tan patch
on sides, white
underside, pale
gray tail stock;
dark line from
flipper to beak;
prominent beak;
tall, moderately
falcate fin;
muted color
pattern.

DIET
Fish and squid.

BREEDING
Probably calves
every 2–3 years;
gestation about
10–11 months.

The long-beaked common dolphin is not as well known as its short-beaked relative. This is partly because it is not as common but also because, until quite recently, it was considered merely as a type of short-beaked common dolphin rather than a separate species in its own right. Now the taxonomists are puzzling over a possible third species, found in the Red Sea, the northern Indian Ocean, and Southeast Asia, which has a similarly long beak but differs in other ways. It has tentatively been named *Delphinus tropicalis*—but its taxonomic status is still uncertain and, in the meantime, it is regarded as a regional variant of the long-beaked. It is not unusual to see schools of long-beaked and short-beaked common dolphins in the same general area on the same day, especially in coastal waters. However, long-beaked seem to prefer shallower and warmer water and usually occur closer to shore. All common dolphins can be distinguished from other dolphins by the unique criss-cross color pattern on their sides.

Where to look

Unlike the short-beaked common dolphin, the long-beaked is usually found close to shore. It lives in warm temperate, subtropical, and tropical waters of the Pacific, Atlantic, and Indian oceans. However, information is fairly limited, because the earlier confusion with short-beaked common dolphins means that many distribution records have not separated the two species. The long-beaked common dolphin is hunted in Peru and possibly elsewhere.

Rough-toothed Dolphin

Steno bredanensis

ID FACT FILE

OTHER NAMES
Slopehead.

MAXIMUM LENGTH
9 feet.

MAXIMUM WEIGHT
350 pounds.

FIELD ID
Slightly robust body; dark, narrow cape; dark and pinkish-white blotches; tall, falcate fin; conical head; long, narrow beak continuous with forehead; white or pinkish-white lips and throat; tip of beak sometimes white; dark patch around eyes.

DIET
Fish, squid, and octopuses.

BREEDING
Calving interval and gestation period unknown.

A strange-looking dolphin with a slightly reptilian appearance, the rough-toothed dolphin is named for a series of fine, vertical wrinkles on the enamel cap of each tooth. Its uniquely sloping forehead, which lacks a crease at the base of the beak, makes it very easy to identify at close range. Many individuals have quite distinctive light-colored blotches, which may be caused by the bites of large squid or cookie-cutter sharks. Rough-toothed dolphins are usually seen in small groups of 10–20 animals, although occasionally there may be as many as 50 traveling together (and one exceptional observation in Hawaii recorded more than 300). They are fairly slow swimmers, but have been known to ride bow waves and perform various aerial behaviors. Often seen in the company of other dolphins, in the eastern tropical Pacific they also associate with flotsam. They have been hunted in many parts of their range, especially in Asia and West Africa, and are almost certainly caught incidentally in fishing nets.

Where to look

Found worldwide in deep oceanic waters of the tropics, subtropics, and some warm temperate regions, the rough-toothed dolphin rarely occurs close to shore except around oceanic islands or where the continental shelf is narrow (although it is frequently encountered in shallow coastal waters in Brazil). With the notable exception of the Maldives, there are relatively few records from the poorly studied Indian Ocean.

Risso's Dolphin
Grampus griseus

ID FACT FILE

OTHER NAMES
Gray dolphin, grampus.

MAXIMUM LENGTH
13 feet.

MAXIMUM WEIGHT
Possibly 1,100 pounds.

FIELD ID
Large, robust body; extensive linear scarring; older animals may appear white; great color variation within school; large, rounded head; indistinct beak; extremely tall fin (relative to body); long, pointed flippers; fin and flippers always dark.

DIET
Mainly squid, some fish, octopuses, and crustaceans.

BREEDING
Calving interval and gestation period unknown.

Risso's dolphins are unmistakable, with their slightly bulging foreheads, remarkably tall dorsal fins, and distinctive battered appearance. The scratches and scars on their bodies are caused mainly by the teeth of other Risso's dolphins, although confrontations with squid may also be to blame. The dorsal fin and flippers always remain dark but their body color tends to lighten with age. Young animals are mainly gray or brown at birth, then darken to nearly black before lightening as they mature. The huge variation in color between individuals within a school—from almost as white as belugas to nearly as dark as pilot whales—is a distinctive feature of Risso's dolphins. Another unique feature, albeit only visible at close range, is a vertical crease down the center of the forehead. Risso's dolphins are usually seen in groups of up to 50 individuals (the average number is 25) but temporary aggregations of hundreds or even several thousand are seen occasionally. They are named after the person who described the type specimen to Georges Cuvier, who formally described the species in 1812.

Where to look

Found worldwide in deep tropical to warm temperate waters, including enclosed seas such as the Mediterranean and Red Sea, Risso's dolphins seem to prefer the steepest edges along the continental shelf. Some individuals may move to higher latitudes during the summer. They are hunted in Sri Lanka, Japan, Indonesia, the Solomon Islands, and Lesser Antilles and are caught incidentally in a wide variety of fishing gear. However, they still seem to be fairly common over much of their range.

Irrawaddy Dolphin

Orcaella brevirostris

ID FACT FILE

OTHER NAMES
Snubfin dolphin.

MAXIMUM LENGTH
9 feet.

MAXIMUM WEIGHT
285 pounds.

FIELD ID
Slender body;
light-gray colored
upperside and
sides, slightly
lighter underside;
large melon;
rounded head
with no beak;
small, stubby
(often triangular)
fin; large,
spatulate
flippers.

DIET
Mainly fish,
some squid,
octopuses,
cuttlefish, and
crustaceans.

BREEDING
Calving interval
unknown;
gestation about
14 months.

A rather unusual dolphin, resembling a small beluga with a dorsal fin, the Irrawaddy dolphin has a strange habit of spitting water from its mouth while spyhopping. Usually quiet and undemonstrative, it tends to be difficult to find in turbid conditions but can sometimes be located by its loud blow. The population off northeastern Australia and Papua New Guinea is unlike other populations, with a lighter, three-toned color pattern, and genetic studies may ultimately prove it to be a separate species (tentatively called the Australian snubfin dolphin, *Orcaella heinsohni*). The Irrawaddy dolphin is revered as a reincarnated human in Laos and Cambodia and some individuals in the Irrawaddy and Mekong rivers cooperate with local fishermen by driving fish into their nets. But elsewhere they are drowned in a variety of fishing nets

and antishark nets, killed by explosive fishing
methods, hunted and captured alive for oceanaria.
Their riverine and coastal habitat is also vulnerable
to human disturbance, damming, pollution, and
industrial development. Consequently, the
Irrawaddy dolphin is believed to be disappearing
from much of its range. It is named after the large
river in Myanmar (formerly Burma).

Where to look

Found in major river systems and shallow coastal
waters (especially mangrove swamps), the Irrawaddy
dolphin lives in
the tropical Indo-
Pacific (from the
western Bay of Bengal to
northern Australia). There are populations in
the Brahmaputra and Ganges, India; Mekong,
Vietnam, Laos, and Cambodia; Mahakam, Borneo;
and Irrawaddy, Myanmar (as far as 810 miles
upstream). It is rarely more than a few miles from
shore. Some individuals probably spend all their
lives in freshwater.

Fraser's Dolphin
Lagenodelphis hosei

ID FACT FILE

OTHER NAMES
White-bellied dolphin, Sarawak dolphin, shortsnout dolphin, Bornean dolphin.

MAXIMUM LENGTH
9 feet.

MAXIMUM WEIGHT
460 pounds.

FIELD ID
Stocky body; blue-gray or gray-brown cape, light gray sides, creamy white or pinkish-white underside; dark lateral stripe; dark stripe from beak, across eyes, to flippers; small, triangular or slightly falcate fin; short but well defined beak; tiny flippers.

DIET
Fish, squid, and crustaceans.

BREEDING
Calves every 2 years; gestation about 12–13 months.

Until the early 1970s, Fraser's dolphin had not been seen alive. But it has been observed many times since and is regularly encountered on dolphin-watching tours in the Caribbean, the Maldives, and elsewhere. It certainly does not seem to be as rare as was once thought. Officially named from a single skull found in 1895 on a beach in Sarawak, on the island of Borneo, it was originally known as the Sarawak dolphin. The British scientist Francis Fraser formally described the species in 1956, giving it the Latin name *Lagenodelphis hosei*. Much later someone gave the dolphin its common name, Fraser's dolphin, to be named after Fraser. The distinctive dark stripes and banditlike facemask are not always present, and vary greatly with age and sex, but at least some individuals in a school of Fraser's dolphins are usually easy to recognize. They tend to live in large schools (typically 100 to 500 but, in some parts of their range, as many as 1,000) and are sometimes seen in the company of melon-headed, false killer, and short-finned pilot whales and several dolphin species.

Where to look

Fraser's dolphin is found worldwide in deep tropical and warm temperate waters, mainly between about 30°N and 30°S. It is rarely seen inshore, except around oceanic islands and in areas with a narrow continental shelf. Significant numbers probably drown in a variety of fishing nets, and relatively small numbers are killed by harpoon and drive fisheries in Asia and elsewhere. A stranding in Brittany, France, was probably a vagrant school.

Common Bottlenose Dolphin

Tursiops truncatus

ID FACT FILE

OTHER NAMES
Bottle-nosed
dolphin, Atlantic
bottlenose
dolphin.

MAXIMUM LENGTH
12 feet 6 inches.

MAXIMUM WEIGHT
1,320 pounds.

FIELD ID
Robust head and
body; subdued
gray or blue-gray
coloring with
darker cape
(indistinct in
many lighting
conditions);
prominent,
falcate fin;
distinct, stubby
beak with
marked melon
crease; rounded
melon.

DIET
Fish, squid,
crustaceans, and
wide variety of
other prey.

BREEDING
Calves every 3–6
years; gestation
12 months.

The bottlenose dolphin is the archetypal
dolphin. It figured prominently in
ancient Greek and Roman mythology
and, more recently, has been the star of
television programs, movies, and marine
parks around the world. It is probably the
species most people imagine when the
word "dolphin" is mentioned and is one
of the most studied and best known of all
the cetaceans. There are many variations,
differing considerably in size, shape, and
color. In particular, there is a smaller,
lighter inshore form and a larger, more
robust offshore form. Inshore animals
tend to live in smaller groups of up to 15
individuals, while it is not unusual to see
groups of several hundred offshore
animals. Wild bottlenose dolphins
(usually males) sometimes become
"friendlies" and seem more interested in
sharing the company of human
swimmers and small boats than of other
dolphins. They also seem to like the
company of other cetaceans, particularly
pilot whales, although can be quite
aggressive toward other species: in the
Moray Firth, Scotland, they are known to
kill harbor porpoises.

COMMON BOTTLENOSE DOLPHIN

Where to look

Common bottlenose dolphins live in tropical to
temperate waters worldwide, close to shore and far
out to sea. They are found in many enclosed seas,
including the Black and Mediterranean Seas
(although the Black
Sea population was
severely depleted
by a fishery which
is now banned).
There is
considerable
overlap in range
with the Indo-
Pacific bottlenose
dolphin. Hunting in
some areas, such as
Japan, Sri Lanka,
the Philippines,
and Chile, may
be a threat to local
populations.

Indo-Pacific Bottlenose Dolphin
Tursiops aduncus

ID FACT FILE

OTHER NAMES
Bottle-nosed dolphin, Pacific bottlenose dolphin, Indian Ocean bottlenose dolphin.

MAXIMUM LENGTH
8 feet 6 inches.

MAXIMUM WEIGHT
510 pounds.

FIELD ID
Slender head and body; subdued gray or blue-gray coloring with darker cape (indistinct in many lighting conditions); dark spots on underside and sides (absent in some individuals); prominent, falcate fin; slender beak with melon crease.

DIET
Fish and squid, some crustaceans and other prey.

BREEDING
Calves every 4–6 years; gestation 12 months.

The possibility of a separate species of bottlenose dolphin, living in the Pacific and Indian Oceans, has been discussed for many years. It was named in 1833 by Ehrenberg and then Rice recognized this species based primarily on the work of LeDuc and Curry. With the help of genetic research the Indo-Pacific bottlenose dolphin was finally given separate species status in the late 1990s, but the major differences between the two have yet to be fully analyzed and described. The Indo-Pacific bottlenose tends to be considerably smaller and less robust, with a longer, more slender beak and proportionally larger dorsal fin and flippers. It also develops dark spots on the underside and sides when it is sexually mature (although spotting is variable between populations and absent from some individuals). The differences between the two species are so significant, despite superficial similarities in their appearance, that the Indo-Pacific bottlenose dolphin may be more closely related to spotted, striped, and spinner dolphins than to its namesake. In some parts of the world it is found in mixed schools with common bottlenose dolphins and other dolphin species such as Indo-Pacific hump-backed.

Where to look

Unlike the common bottlenose, the Indo-Pacific bottlenose dolphin is found only in shallow coastal waters, which makes it particularly vulnerable to human disturbance and environmental degradation. However, there is considerable overlap in the ranges of the two species. The Indo-Pacific bottlenose lives in tropical and subtropical regions of the western Pacific and around the rim of the Indian Ocean as far as the southern tip of Africa.

Commerson's Dolphin

Cephalorhynchus commersonii

ID FACT FILE

OTHER NAMES
Skunk dolphin, piebald dolphin, black-and-white dolphin.

MAXIMUM LENGTH
5 feet 6 inches.

MAXIMUM WEIGHT
200 pounds.

FIELD ID
Small, stocky body; black-and-white coloration (black and gray in Kerguelen); inconspicuous beak; conical head with gently-sloping forehead; rounded flippers; low-profile, broadly-rounded fin; black flippers, flukes and fin.

DIET
Mainly fish and crustaceans.

BREEDING
Calving interval unknown; gestation about 12 months.

A striking animal, with a stocky body and distinctive black-and-white markings, Commerson's dolphin is one of the smallest oceanic dolphins. It looks rather like a porpoise, but is very dolphinlike in its behavior—a fast and active swimmer, it frequently rides the bow-waves of passing boats and is an enthusiastic breacher. It can often be seen swimming upside down, spinning underwater as it goes, and seems to enjoy surfing in breakers close to shore. There is considerable variation in appearance from one individual to another, particularly in the extent of black and white. There is also a possible subspecies living around Kerguelen Island, in the Indian Ocean, which is significantly larger than its South American counterpart, has a better-defined beak and is black, white, and gray rather than black and white. Commerson's dolphin is named after a French scientist, Philibert Commerson, who sent the first description back to Europe after observing it in the Strait of Magellan in 1767.

Where to look
Commerson's dolphin is found in shallow coastal
waters, with the main center of distribution in
cold temperate and subantarctic waters around
southern Argentina, the extreme south of Chile in
Tierra del Fuego, and the Falkland Islands. There
is also an apparently isolated population around
Kerguelen Island in the Indian Ocean—more
than 5,000 miles away. Commerson's dolphins were
hunted for use as crab bait in Chile and Argentina
(now illegal) and are vulnerable to drownings in gill
nets.

Hector's Dolphin

Cephalorhynchus hectori

ID FACT FILE

OTHER NAMES
New Zealand
dolphin, little
pied dolphin.

MAXIMUM LENGTH
5 feet.

MAXIMUM WEIGHT
132 pounds.

FIELD ID
Small, stocky
body; rounded
fin; conical head
with no beak;
complex color
pattern (gray
forehead, light
gray upperside
and sides, white
underside with
finger-shaped
lobe pointing
toward tail);
broad black band
across eye to
flipper.

DIET
Fish and squid,
some
crustaceans.

BREEDING
Calves every 2–4
years; gestation
about 10–11
months.

Hector's dolphin is one of the smallest of all dolphins. A distinctive little animal, with a broad, black, rounded dorsal fin, it is found only in New Zealand. It can appear dark from a distance, but at close range has a striking, complex color pattern of gray, black, and white. It often bow-rides, especially in front of small, slow-moving boats, and is playful and acrobatic. Large numbers of Hector's dolphins are drowned in coastal gill nets, which may have reduced the population by more than half since the early 1970s. The Banks Peninsula Marine Mammal Sanctuary was established in 1989 to protect a key area of 452 square miles from commercial gill-netting and this has helped (but not entirely solved) the problem locally. In recent years, high-speed boats have been posing another serious threat. Hector's dolphin is now an endangered species. There could be as few as 100 individuals surviving around North Island and the population around South Island is numbered in low thousands.

Where to look
Found only in New Zealand, Hector's dolphin lives
in shallow coastal waters mainly off South Island
(there are two genetically distinct subpopulations:
one off the west coast and the other off the east and
south coasts). There is also a small remnant
population along the west coast of North Island. It
rarely ventures more than six miles offshore in
summer (usually just beyond the surf line or in
harbors), but at least some disperse further offshore
during winter.

Heaviside's Dolphin

Cephalorhynchus heavisidii

ID FACT FILE

OTHER NAMES
Benguela
dolphin, South
African dolphin.

MAXIMUM LENGTH
6 feet.

MAXIMUM WEIGHT
165 pounds.

FIELD ID
Small, stocky
body; gray
anterior, dark
posterior; white
belly with lobes;
gray, cone-
shaped head;
indistinct beak;
dark patch
around eye;
prominent
triangular fin
about midway
along back; dark
flippers, fin, and
flukes; small
groups of fewer
than 10 typical.

DIET
Variety of coastal
fish, squid, and
octopus.

BREEDING
Possible calves
every 2–4 years;
gestation may be
10–11 months.

The enigmatic Heaviside's dolphin has long been shrouded in mystery. Our limited knowledge of this distinctive, porpoiselike dolphin is based mostly on opportunistic encounters rather than detailed studies. Even its name is rather confusing. It should have been named after Captain Haviside, who brought the first specimen from Africa to England in 1827, but was mistakenly named after Captain Heaviside, an eminent surgeon who collected anatomical specimens. However, in recent years there have been regular tours to see Heaviside's dolphins from Lambert's Bay, South Africa, and Walvis Bay, Namibia, offering a unique opportunity for some thrilling close encounters. True acrobats, the dolphins are thoroughly at home in turbulent water close to shore and can often be seen surfing or playing in the waves. They frequently leap high into the air, sometimes turning complete somersaults, and are keen bow-riders. Little is known about the status of Heaviside's dolphins, although unknown numbers are drowned in coastal fishing nets and there is evidence of limited hunting for their meat in some areas.

Where to look

Heaviside's dolphin has a very restricted range in shallow, coastal waters of South Africa and Namibia. It occurs from near the Angola–Namibia border (at about 17°S) south to Cape Point, South Africa (at about 34°S). It is normally within a few miles of shore in water less than 330 feet deep, but has been encountered 50 miles offshore in water 600 feet deep. It seems to be associated with the cold, northward-flowing Benguela Current.

Chilean Dolphin

Cephalorhynchus eutropia

ID FACT FILE

OTHER NAMES
White-bellied
dolphin, black
dolphin.

MAXIMUM LENGTH
6 feet.

MAXIMUM WEIGHT
145 pounds.

FIELD ID
Small, stocky
body; subtle dark
pigmentation on
upperside and
sides, white
underside
(including throat);
conical head with
indistinct beak;
pale gray
forehead; white
lips; large,
rounded fin.

DIET
Fish, squid, and
crustaceans.

BREEDING
Possibly calves
every 2–4 years;
gestation about
10–11 months.

The Chilean dolphin tends to be quite a shy animal, particularly in the southern part of its range. One of the smallest of all cetaceans, it is known from a mixed collection of skeletons, a handful of strandings, and an increasing number of reliable sightings. It can appear all black at sea, but has a complex and rather subtle pigmentation of light and dark gray on the back and sides and a distinctive white belly and throat. However, the body color darkens very quickly after death and this may account for its original name—the black dolphin—and for some of the inaccurate descriptions in early reports. The Chilean dolphin normally lives in small groups of two or three animals, although as many as 50 have been observed together and historical records report schools of several thousand. It is known to bow-ride in the north of its range, but hunting has made it wary in the south. It is hunted illegally for crab bait, and unknown numbers drown in coastal gill nets. The total population is probably numbered in low thousands.

Where to look

As its name suggests, the Chilean dolphin is found mainly in the cold, shallow, coastal waters of Chile. It lives along both open and sheltered coasts, from near Cape Horn (55°S) in the south to Valparaíso (about 33°S) in the north. It may sometimes occur at the extreme southern tip of Argentina, as well. It frequently enters small channels, estuaries, and rivers, and seems to prefer areas with rapid tidal flow or turbulent water.

Hourglass Dolphin

Lagenorhynchus cruciger

ID FACT FILE

OTHER NAMES
Sea skunk.

MAXIMUM LENGTH
6 feet.

MAXIMUM WEIGHT
210 pounds.

FIELD ID
Small, stocky body; sharply-demarcated black, white, and gray markings; rough hourglass pattern on sides; short, black beak; large, falcate fin (variable in shape); black flippers, fin, and flukes; fast swimmer.

DIET
Fish and squid, some crustaceans.

BREEDING
Calving interval and gestation period unknown.

Named for the crude black-and-white hourglass pattern on its sides, the hourglass dolphin is an inhabitant of remote Antarctic and sub-Antarctic seas. It has not been studied in detail and was originally named in 1824 from little more than rough drawings made at sea. Incredibly, no more than 20 specimens have been collected since. However, it is frequently encountered by cruise ships in the Drake Passage on their way to and from the Antarctic Peninsula, and seems to enjoy riding in their bow-waves and stern-waves. Its striking body markings—and the fact that it is the only dolphin with a dorsal fin consistently found in the open waters of the Southern Ocean—make it relatively easy to identify. Sometimes seen in association with fin whales, long-finned pilot whales, southern rightwhale dolphins, and other cetaceans, and under large gatherings of feeding seabirds, hourglass dolphins usually live in small groups of about four to seven animals (although schools of more than 100 have been recorded). Limited evidence suggests that there may be a population of about 140,000 south of the Antarctic Convergence.

Where to look
The hourglass dolphin is found in high latitudes of the southern hemisphere, both north and south of the Antarctic Convergence, mainly between 45°S and 60°S. It is predominantly oceanic, but sometimes ventures right up to the ice-edge and may be encountered relatively close to shore in places like the South Shetland Islands. It has never been systematically exploited.

Peale's Dolphin
Lagenorhynchus australis

ID FACT FILE

OTHER NAMES
Blackchin
dolphin.

MAXIMUM LENGTH
7 feet.

MAXIMUM WEIGHT
Possibly 255
pounds.

FIELD ID
Robust body;
dark back with
single grayish-
white streak on
each side;
grayish-white
sides, white
underside;
predominantly
dark face and
chin; white
"armpits";
short, indistinct
beak; tall,
predominantly
grayish-black,
falcate fin.

DIET
Fish, squid,
octopuses, and
crustaceans.

BREEDING
Calving interval
and gestation
period unknown.

Peale's dolphin resembles a dusky dolphin in overall appearance, but it has some distinctive features of its own, in particular, a dark face and brilliant white "armpits." Found only in southern South America and the Falkland Islands, it is sometimes described as an "entrance dolphin" because it tends to be found in tide rips at the entrance to fjords and channels. Peale's dolphins are often observed swimming in shallow water parallel to shore, in small groups of about two to five animals (although as many as 100 have been seen together). They usually travel quite slowly, but will ride the bow-waves of large vessels or swim alongside smaller ones, and are perfectly capable of breaching and spyhopping. They often associate with Commerson's dolphins, which overlap in range. Peale's dolphins have been heavily exploited for use as bait in crab traps in southern Chile since at least the early 1970s and there has been a marked decrease in numbers in some areas. The scale of the hunting has declined, mainly because fishing effort is now directed more at sea urchins and less at crabs, but unknown numbers of dolphins are still being harpooned.

Where to look

Found in the coastal waters and over shallow
continental shelves of southern South America,
between about 38°S in the Pacific and 44°S in the
Atlantic, Peale's dolphins are often associated with
swiftly flowing water. Frequently seen around the
Falkland Islands and Tierra del Fuego, they often
greet returning Antarctic cruise ships as they
approach Cape Horn. They are frequently found in
association with kelp beds.

Atlantic White-sided Dolphin

Lagenorhynchus acutus

ID FACT FILE

OTHER NAMES
Lag, white-side, jumper, springer.

MAXIMUM LENGTH
9 feet.

MAXIMUM WEIGHT
510 pounds.

FIELD ID
Robust body with thick tail stock; black or dark gray upperside, gray stripe along flanks, white underside (extends onto side above flipper); white patch below fin and yellow or tan streak along each side of tail stock; short, thick beak; tall, falcate fin.

DIET
Fish and squid.

BREEDING
Calves every 2 years; gestation 11 months.

At first glance, the striking yellow or tan streak along each side of the Atlantic white-sided dolphin makes it look superficially similar to a common dolphin. But the position of the streak on the tail stock, and the complex and sharply demarcated pattern of bold gray, white, and black on the rest of the body, make it quite a distinctive species at close

range. It is certainly one of the most colorful of all the world's dolphins. The Atlantic white-sided dolphin is a gregarious species, typically living in cohesive groups of between five and 50 (depending on the location) or looser aggregations of 500 or more. It often feeds in association with fin, humpback, and other large whales, sometimes even riding their bow-waves, and will swim alongside slow ships and boats or bow-ride in front of faster ones.

Researchers often call it a "lag," which is short for the scientific name *Lagenorhynchus*. A very rough population estimate of a few hundred thousand has been made for the entire North Atlantic.

Where to look
Atlantic white-sided dolphins are found in cold temperate and subarctic waters of the northern North Atlantic, especially over the continental shelf and slope. Their range is remarkably similar to that of the white-beaked dolphin, with a band from northern Europe, through southern Greenland to Newfoundland, Nova Scotia, and down the north-east coast of the States to Cape Cod. Several hundred get caught up and killed in the Faroese pilot whale hunt every year.

Pacific White-sided Dolphin

Lagenorhynchus obliquidens

ID FACT FILE

OTHER NAMES
Lag, Pacific striped dolphin.

MAXIMUM LENGTH
8 feet.

MAXIMUM WEIGHT
400 pounds.

FIELD ID
Robust body; black or dark gray upperside, white underside; large pale gray patch above flippers; bold black line demarcating white belly; pale gray streak on sides; bicolored fin and flippers; indistinct black-tipped beak; tall, broad-based, falcate fin.

DIET
Fish and squid.

BREEDING
Possibly calves every 2–3 years; gestation about 12 months.

Pacific white-sided dolphins are great fun to watch. They often live in large schools containing hundreds or even thousands of individuals and are so lively and boisterous that their splashes can be seen long before it is possible to see the animals themselves. They leap into the air and spin or turn complete somersaults before splashing back into the water, and often ride the bow waves of passing boats or ships. Seen from above when they are bow-riding, the two narrow stripes down each side look like a pair of suspenders and are very distinctive. Pacific white-sided dolphins look remarkably similar to dusky dolphins and it has been suggested that the two belong to the same species; however, genetic evidence does not support this idea and there is no overlap in range. Like their Atlantic counterparts, they are gregarious animals and they can often be seen with other cetaceans, especially Risso's dolphins and northern rightwhale dolphins, as well as sea lions and seals. Researchers often call them "lags," which is short for the scientific name *Lagenorhynchus*.

Where to look

Found in cold temperate waters across the northern North Pacific, this fairly abundant species occurs mainly offshore or in very deep water closer to shore. Huge numbers were killed in drift-net fisheries on the high seas until this type of fishing was banned in 1993, but hundreds still die in fishing nets set within the 200-nautical-mile limits of some countries. The total population could be as high as one million.

Dusky Dolphin

Lagenorhynchus obscurus

ID FACT FILE

OTHER NAMES
None.

MAXIMUM LENGTH
7 feet.

MAXIMUM WEIGHT
200 pounds.

FIELD ID
Small, robust body; predominantly dark upperside, white underside; two forward-pointing white or pale gray blazes along sides; prominent, falcate, two-toned fin; short, thick, dark beak; predominantly white face; small black patch around each eye.

DIET
Fish and squid.

BREEDING
Calving interval unknown; gestation 11–13 months.

Dusky dolphins are social animals and seem to welcome the company of other species as well as their own. They frequently associate with a wide variety of whales and dolphins, as well as seals, a range of seabirds, and even people. Very inquisitive animals, they frequently approach boats and sometimes play with people in the water. Well known for their high leaps and somersaults, "duskies" are incredibly acrobatic; they often repeat their aerial displays dozens of times in a row and, when one animal starts, others may follow suit. Their group size varies from as few as 15 animals to as many as 500; larger gatherings tend to separate into small subgroups to feed, but these join forces to socialize and rest. Duskies are remarkably similar to Pacific white-sided dolphins in appearance, although there is no overlap in range. In Peru, as many as 10,000 of them were killed every year during the mid-1980s. The hunting of dolphins has been banned there since 1993, but significant numbers are still being harpooned. Unknown, but probably significant, numbers drown in fishing nets throughout their range.

Where to look

Widely scattered in temperate waters throughout the southern hemisphere, the dusky dolphin is generally found in coastal and shelf waters. There are three main populations, in South America (including the Falkland Islands), southwestern Africa, and New Zealand (including Chatham, Auckland, and Campbell Islands), as well as around several oceanic islands. It seems to be more abundant in the northern parts of its range in winter and in the southern parts in summer.

White-beaked Dolphin

Lagenorhynchus albirostris

ID FACT FILE

OTHER NAMES
Squidhound.

MAXIMUM LENGTH
10 feet.

MAXIMUM WEIGHT
770 pounds.

FIELD ID
Very robust body;
predominantly
dark upperside,
white underside;
grayish-white
streak on each
side; pale area
on tail stock;
short, thick beak
(usually white,
but may be
brown or gray);
dark flippers, fin
and flukes; very
prominent fin.

DIET
Fish, squid,
octopuses, and
crustaceans.

BREEDING
Calving interval
unknown;
gestation 10–11
months.

Despite its name, the white-beaked dolphin does not always have a white beak—it can be white, brown, light gray, or dark gray. Despite some exceptions there is evidence to suggest that more animals have white beaks in the east of the range, and fewer in the west. The two populations are morphologically distinct and it is likely that they rarely mix. The rather diffuse body pattern of white, gray, and black is also highly variable between individuals. Strikingly large and robust for a dolphin, the white-beaked is capable of swimming at considerable speed and is frequently very acrobatic. It can sometimes be seen feeding with fin and humpback whales, and with other dolphin species. No detailed abundance estimates have been made, but there are likely to be many tens of thousands (if not hundreds of thousands) across the North Atlantic. It tends to be more common in Europe than in North America.

Where to look

Found farther north than any other dolphin, the white-beaked dolphin is widely distributed in cool temperate and subarctic waters of the northern North Atlantic. Its distribution is broadly similar to that of the Atlantic white-sided dolphin, although it occurs farther into the Barents Sea and higher up both coasts of Greenland. Found mainly over the continental shelf, and also occasionally in shallow coastal waters.

Franciscana
Pontoporia blainvillei

ID FACT FILE

OTHER NAMES
La Plata dolphin.

MAXIMUM LENGTH
6 feet.

MAXIMUM WEIGHT
120 pounds.

FIELD ID
Small body; gray or brown upperside and sides, lighter underside; extremely long, slender beak; bulging melon; broad, almost triangular flippers; rounded, slightly triangular fin set behind midpoint on back.

DIET
Mainly fish, some squid, octopuses, and crustaceans.

BREEDING
Calves every 2 years; gestation 10–11 months.

Despite its classification as a river dolphin, the franciscana lives in the sea and prefers shallow estuarine or coastal waters. It is believed to feed mostly at or near the seabed, probing for food and even pulling away vegetation in its search for suitable prey. An undemonstrative and inconspicuous animal that seems to spend much of its life alone, it is easy to overlook in anything but the calmest conditions. Consequently, it is poorly known. It is one of the smallest of all cetaceans and yet has the longest beak (relative to body size) of any dolphin. The beak of the juvenile is considerably shorter than that of the adult, but its relative length increases as the animal grows older. There are no distinctive color markings —franciscanas are generally gray in the north of their range and slightly browner in the south. They are sometimes called La Plata dolphins, because the first specimen (described in 1844) was found in the Río de la Plata estuary, shared by Uruguay and Argentina. Significant numbers have been drowned in fishing nets since World War II and, living close to shore, they are particularly susceptible to habitat disturbance and pollution.

Where to look

Found in temperate coastal waters of eastern South America, the franciscana is known from Itaúnas in Espiritu Santo, Brazil, south to the northern coast of Golfo San Matías, in northern Patagonia, Argentina. Although it is common in the La Plata estuary, and some other estuaries, it does not travel upriver. It rarely ventures more than 35 miles offshore and is usually found in water that is less than 100 feet deep.

Baiji
Lipotes vexillifer

ID FACT FILE

OTHER NAMES
Yangtze river dolphin, beiji, pei c'hi, whitefin dolphin, whiteflag dolphin, Chinese river dolphin.

MAXIMUM LENGTH
8 feet.

MAXIMUM WEIGHT
375 pounds.

FIELD ID
Robust body; small head with rounded melon; bluish-gray upperside and sides, grayish-white or white underside; subtle, diffuse color variations on face; long, narrow beak slightly upturned at tip; very low, triangular fin; tiny eyes; broad flippers.

DIET
Fish.

BREEDING
Calving interval unknown; gestation possibly 10–11 months.

The Baiji is the rarest and most endangered cetacean in the world. There were about 400 survivors in 1979–1980, 200 in 1986, fewer than 100 in 1989–1991, and no more than a couple dozen in 1998. No one knows exactly how many are left today, but there could be as few as 10 or 20—or the species could already be extinct. An estimated 12 percent of the entire human population lives in the basin of the dolphin's home in the Yangtze River, China, so it faces an inordinate number of threats. Dangerous fishing hooks, overfishing, heavy boat traffic, pollution, riverbank development, and dam construction contrive to ensure that it is almost certainly doomed in its natural home. A single captive male called Qi-Qi (pronounced chee-chee)

was a crucial source of information for many years. He was rescued in 1980, after being injured by fishing hooks, and remained in captivity until his death, aged about 24, on July 14, 2002. At present, the future for the Yangtze river dolphin looks bleaker than ever.

Where to look
Until recently, the Baiji was found mainly in the middle and lower reaches of the Yangtze River, in China (along a 1,056-mile stretch from the mouth of the river). Its presence in the Yangtze was recorded as long as 2,000 years ago. Now absent from most or all of its former range, it has always preferred areas where tributaries enter the river, especially immediately upstream or downstream of sandbanks or islets.

Indus River Dolphin

Platanista minor

ID FACT FILE

OTHER NAMES
Blind river
dolphin, bhulan.

MAXIMUM LENGTH
8 feet.

MAXIMUM WEIGHT
187 pounds.

FIELD ID
Robust body;
uniform gray or
gray-brown color
(sometimes with
pinkish
underside); long,
narrow beak
(thickens and
opens slightly
toward tip); low,
triangular hump
instead of fin;
small head with
rounded melon;
tiny eyes;
sneezelike blow.

DIET
Fish and
crustaceans.

BREEDING
Calving interval
unknown;
gestation
possibly 12
months.

There has been considerable
uncertainty about the status of Indus
and Ganges river dolphins for many
years. Although living in different river
systems, and therefore separated
geographically, they look almost
identical and have remarkably similar
habits. First they were believed to be
the same species; then, in the 1970s,
differences in the structure of their
skulls and blood protein composition
were discovered, and it was decided
that they were two separate species. But
the study sample was very small and it
has all been thrown into doubt again, so
now many experts consider them to be
subspecies: *Platanista gangetica minor*
and *Platanista gangetica gangetica*. Like
its close relative, the Indus river dolphin
is normally found in very turbid, silt-

laden waters, and does not enter the sea. It is one of the most endangered cetaceans in the world and, until recently, was thought to be dangerously close to extinction. However, a recent survey estimated a total surviving population of at least 1,000. This is still not many but is considerably more than the low hundreds once feared.

Where to look

Found exclusively in the Indus River, in the Pakistani provinces of Sind and Punjab, the Indus river dolphin has been split into isolated pockets by dams and barrages built for irrigation and hydroelectric power generation. The majority of the population now lives at the downstream end of the range, between the Guddu and Sukkur barrages. They tend to congregate in the main channels during the dry season, dispersing into swollen creeks and minor tributaries during the monsoon.

Ganges River Dolphin

Platanista gangetica

ID FACT FILE

OTHER NAMES
Ganges susu, blind river dolphin, Gangetic dolphin.

MAXIMUM LENGTH
8 feet.

MAXIMUM WEIGHT
187 pounds.

FIELD ID
Robust body; uniform gray or gray-brown color (sometimes with pinkish underside); long, narrow beak (thickens and opens slightly toward tip); low, triangular hump instead of fin; small head with rounded melon; tiny eyes; sneezelike blow.

DIET
Fish and crustaceans.

BREEDING
Calving interval unknown; gestation possibly 12 months.

The Ganges and Indus river dolphins are the only cetaceans without a crystalline lens in their eyes. Their retinas have light-gathering receptors, so they can probably detect the direction (and perhaps intensity) of light. But for all intents and purposes they are blind. Instead, they find their way around and catch food in their turbid riverine homes by building up a "sound picture" of their surroundings, in much the same way that a bat navigates in the dark. They have an unusual swimming behavior, which involves turning on one side, nodding the head, and perhaps

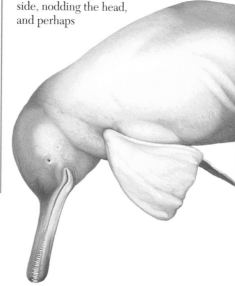

trailing a flipper in the mud to search for food. Both species can be difficult to find, but listen for their blows which, on calm days, can often be heard from very far away. The Hindi name of the Ganges river dolphin, "susu," is meant to imitate the sneezelike sound made when they breathe. Both species face a great many threats, including entanglement in fishing gear, hunting, pollution, and dam and barrage construction. There is no reliable population estimate for the Ganges river dolphin, but it is probably in the low thousands.

Where to look

More widely distributed than its close relative in the Indus, the Ganges river dolphin is found in the Ganges, Meghna, and Brahmaputra river systems of western India, Bangladesh, Nepal, and Bhutan, and the Karnaphuli and Sangu rivers of Bangladesh. However, it is now virtually extinct in Nepal. Dams and barrages have fragmented the population throughout its range.

Amazon River Dolphin

Inia geoffrensis

ID FACT FILE

OTHER NAMES
Boto, pink
dolphin.

MAXIMUM LENGTH
8 feet.

MAXIMUM WEIGHT
400 pounds.

FIELD ID
Long, rather
stocky body; vivid
pink, bluish-gray
or off-white color;
low, humplike fin
and long ridge
toward tail; very
long beak;
bulbous melon
(shape can be
changed at will);
flexible neck;
large, triangular
flippers.

DIET
Mainly fish,
some
invertebrates
and small
turtles.

BREEDING
Calving interval
unknown;
gestation 10–11
months.

A strange-looking animal, with a pinkish body and enormous flippers, the Amazon river dolphin tends to be more playful than its closest relatives. It can be inquisitive and will sometimes approach boats or people in the water and has even been known to toss turtles into the air and grab fishermen's paddles. This is the largest of the river dolphins and, in the right areas, is the easiest to see. It often associates with the tucuxi, the only other cetacean in the Amazon Basin, and sometimes shares feeding grounds with giant otters. Its pinkish color is caused by blood flow and becomes more accentuated when the animal is excited or aroused, but it is highly variable according to age, water clarity, temperature, and location. There are three recognized subspecies, and they are found in the Amazon River basin, the Madeira River basin, and the Orinoco River basin. The Amazon river dolphin is the most abundant of the world's river dolphins, with an estimated population numbered in tens of thousands, but it is facing many threats common to all river dolphins, as well as deforestation in its rainforest home.

Where to look

Found in all the main rivers of the Amazon and Orinoco basins (in Brazil, Colombia, Venezuela, Ecuador, Guyana, Peru, and Bolivia), the Amazon river dolphin occurs more than 1,865 miles inland in some areas. In the dry season it is confined to the main rivers and tributaries, but in the rainy season it frequently enters flooded jungles and grasslands, swimming between the trees.

Vaquita
Phocoena sinus

ID FACT FILE

OTHER NAMES
Gulf of California porpoise, cochito.

MAXIMUM LENGTH
5 feet.

MAXIMUM WEIGHT
120 pounds.

FIELD ID
Very small size; stocky body shape; complex but subtle gray cape, lighter gray sides, white underside; prominent, dolphinlike fin; virtually no beak; rounded head; dark patch around each eye; dark stripe from corner of beak to flipper.

DIET
Fish and squid, some crustaceans.

BREEDING
Calves every year; gestation possibly 10–11 months.

One of the rarest and most endangered marine cetaceans in the world, the vaquita is very poorly known. Even on official surveys around its home in the northern Sea of Cortez, this very small porpoise often eludes professional biologists for days or even weeks at a time.

It either avoids or ignores boats and shows very little of itself at the surface. Consequently, few people have ever seen the species alive and we know little about its life and habits. At a recent conference, one vaquita researcher made a dismal prediction: "probably in less than 10 years the vaquita will be extinct." Others are not quite as pessimistic, but its future is undoubtedly bleak. There are some 500–600 vaquitas left and an estimated 39–84 are believed to drown in gill nets every year. This is a huge number considering the small size of the surviving population. The Mexican government established the Upper Gulf of California and Colorado River Delta Biosphere Reserve in 1993, but some 40 percent of the vaquita population lives outside this protected area. More stringent conservation efforts are needed urgently if it is to survive.

Where to look

The vaquita probably has the most restricted distribution of any marine cetacean. It survives only in the extreme northern end of the Sea of Cortez (Gulf of California) in western Mexico (north of 30°45'N). Most common around the Colorado River Delta, it is usually seen within 7–15 miles of shore and is rarely encountered in water much deeper than 130 feet (usually 36–165 feet.)

Harbor Porpoise

Phocoena phocoena

ID FACT FILE

OTHER NAMES
Common porpoise, puffing pig, puffer.

MAXIMUM LENGTH
6 feet.

MAXIMUM WEIGHT
175 pounds.

FIELD ID
Small size; robust body; nondescript coloring (gray upperside, lighter sides and underside); triangular fin (large relative to visible portion of back when surfacing); indistinct beak; small, conical head; one or more dark stripes from mouth to flipper.

DIET
Mainly fish, some squid and octopuses; crustaceans (calves only).

BREEDING
Calves every 1–2 years; gestation 10–11 months.

The harbor porpoise is the most widespread and commonly seen of all the porpoises. However, it is generally wary of boats and rarely bow-rides. A brief glimpse of its dark back and low, triangular dorsal fin is all this undemonstrative little cetacean usually shows of itself. When it rises to breathe, the lasting impression is of a slow, forward-rolling motion, as if the dorsal fin is mounted on a revolving wheel lifted briefly above the surface and then withdrawn. As with most dolphins and porpoises, its blow is rarely seen. However, it can sometimes be heard and sounds something like a sneeze, giving the harbor porpoise one of its alternative names, the puffing pig. Like all porpoises, it has spade-shaped teeth— quite unlike the conical teeth of dolphins. Once hunted intensively in Europe for its meat and blubber (especially in the seventeenth and eighteenth centuries), it is now protected in most of its range. However, the biggest threat to harbor porpoises today is incidental capture in gill nets, herring weirs, and other fishing equipment, which drown many thousands every year.

Where to look

Found in cool temperate and subarctic waters of the
northern hemisphere, the harbor porpoise is usually
seen within 6 miles of land. It frequents relatively
shallow bays, estuaries, and tidal channels less than
about 650 feet in depth. There are three distinct
populations, which are reproductively isolated and
classified as separate subspecies. They live in the
North Atlantic, the North Pacific, and the Black Sea.

Burmeister's Porpoise

Phocoena spinipinnis

ID FACT FILE

OTHER NAMES
Black porpoise.

MAXIMUM LENGTH
6 feet.

MAXIMUM WEIGHT
230 pounds.

FIELD ID
Small, stocky
body;
predominantly
dark gray or
black, lighter
underside;
backward-leaning
fin (farther back
than on any
other small
cetacean);
conical head;
flattened
forehead;
indistinct beak;
dark eye patch;
dark gray stripe
from chin to
flipper.

DIET
Mainly fish,
some squid and
crustaceans.

BREEDING
Probably calves
every 1–2 years;
gestation 11–12
months.

Easily recognized by its small size and backward-pointing dorsal fin, Burmeister's porpoise is nevertheless rather inconspicuous and rarely seen. It will often accelerate and swim away when approached by a boat. However, it is believed to be considerably more abundant than the limited number of sightings would otherwise suggest, especially in the Strait of Magellan and Beagle Channel, around Tierra del Fuego. The dorsal fin is unique among cetaceans—it really does look as if it is leaning backward, pointing toward the tail, and has a series of small tubercles (knoblike prominences) on the leading edge that become sharper as the animal grows older. Typically seen alone or in pairs (with occasional temporary aggregations of eight or more), Burmeister's porpoises normally appear completely dark at sea. Hundreds or even thousands of them are hunted for human food and bait every year, especially in Peru and Chile, and they are believed to be caught and drowned in a variety of fishing nets throughout much of their range.

Where to look

Burmeister's porpoise is found in the shallow coastal waters of South America. Its range extends from Cape Horn north as far as Bahía de Paita, in northern Peru, on the Pacific side and as far as Santa Catarine, in southern Brazil, on the Atlantic side. Limited evidence suggests that it is most common close to shore in summer (sometimes inside the kelp line and even in the lower reaches of rivers) and up to 30 miles offshore in winter.

Finless Porpoise
Neophocaena phocaenoides

ID FACT FILE

OTHER NAMES
Black porpoise,
black finless
porpoise,
jiangzhu.

MAXIMUM LENGTH
6 feet 6 inches.

MAXIMUM WEIGHT
198 pounds.

FIELD ID
Very small size;
slender body;
pale blue-gray or
gray body color,
slightly paler
underside;
dorsal ridge but
no fin; small
head and no
beak; rounded
melon; long,
pointed flippers;
good head
mobility.

DIET
Fish, squid,
octopuses,
cuttlefish, and
crustaceans.

BREEDING
Probably calves
every 2 years;
gestation about
11 months.

One of the smallest of all cetaceans, the finless porpoise is the only porpoise without a dorsal fin and, consequently, looks rather like a small beluga. Instead of a fin it has a long ridge with a line of circular bumps, known as tubercles, which may be used by the female as an antislip device to "carry" its calf. Despite two of its alternative names, it is normally a pale blue-gray color (though some populations darken with age and they often turn black

after death). It is the only porpoise in the region, apart from a slight overlap in range with harbor porpoises in Japan and the Sea of Japan. Finless porpoises are usually difficult to observe, rarely leaping from the water and never bow-riding, but some populations are more approachable. In fact, there are even commercial trips to see them in northern Kyushu, Japan. The species has virtually disappeared from much of its former range, mainly because of incidental capture in fishing nets. It also suffers for living close to shore—from pollution, overfishing, deforestation of mangrove swamps, and disturbance.

Where to look
Finless porpoises are found in warm, coastal waters and some major river systems in the Indo-Pacific.

Their range stretches from the Persian Gulf to northern Japan and down to Java (and, possibly, to New Guinea and northern Australia). They are rarely more than a few miles from land and occur in both saltwater and freshwater. One of the best-known populations lives in the Yangtze River, China, where they are found up to 1,000 miles from the sea.

Spectacled Porpoise
Phocoena dioptrica

ID FACT FILE

OTHER NAMES
None.

MAXIMUM LENGTH
7 feet.

MAXIMUM WEIGHT
250 pounds.

FIELD ID
Small, robust
body; jet-black
upperside, white
underside; male
has high rounded
fin, female has
lower, more
triangular fin;
small, rounded
head with no
beak; black eye
patch with white
"spectacles";
black lips.

DIET
Fish and
crustaceans,
possibly squid.

BREEDING
Calving interval
and gestation
period unknown.

Named for the fine white line around each eye, the spectacled porpoise is rarely seen even in its apparent stronghold along the wild, Atlantic beaches of Tierra del Fuego, at the extreme southern tip of South America. Until 1976, the species was known from only nine

specimens and one sighting and even today most information comes from weathered bones and carcasses washed ashore. The striking, clearly demarcated markings of jet black and white are distinctive. Interestingly, the two sexes are very different in appearance. The male has a large, rounded dorsal fin, while the female's is much smaller and more triangular in shape. There has long been confusion over its taxonomy. It was originally placed in the genus *Phocoena* with most of the other porpoises, then in the mid-1980s was placed in a separate genus, *Australophocaena*, but recently it was returned to *Phocoena*. Remains of spectacled porpoises have been found in

6,000-year-old kitchen middens of the canoe people in Tierra del Fuego. Little is known about the threats they face today, but they certainly drown in gill nets and trawls.

Where to look

Known mostly from cold temperate and subantarctic waters around the southern Atlantic coast of South America and New Zealand and Australia, the spectacled porpoise is found in both coastal and offshore waters. Its distribution appears to be circumpolar because there are records from widely separate islands across the southern hemisphere, including the Falklands, South Georgia, Kerguelen, Heard, Macquarie, and Auckland.

Dall's Porpoise

Phocoenoides dalli

Dall's porpoise is the fastest of the small cetaceans and is usually seen as a blur when it breaks the surface at high speed. It produces a distinctive spray of water called the "rooster tail," which is made by a cone of water coming off the head as it rises to breathe and can almost obscure the animal itself. It is a very distinctive porpoise, with an exceptionally stocky body and striking markings, which are mostly black but with brilliant white patches on the sides and underside. There are two distinct forms. The Dalli-type occurs throughout the range and has a smaller area of white on the flanks. The Truei-type, which is found only in the western North Pacific, has more white. Unlike most other porpoises, it often approaches boats and readily bow-rides (although it soon loses interest in vessels traveling too slowly). Huge numbers are killed by drift-net fisheries and large numbers die in a variety of other fishing equipment. Nearly 20,000 are killed every year in Japan to provide meat for human consumption. The total population is probably in the order of several hundred thousand.

Where to look

Dall's porpoises live in the cool temperate waters of
the North Pacific, and adjacent seas (Bering Sea,
Okhotsk Sea, and Sea of Japan). They are mainly
oceanic but are found close to shore where the
water is sufficiently deep, such as over deep-water
canyons. There may be a seasonal shift in some
areas because they are found north and offshore in
summer, south and inshore in winter.

SPECIES CHECKLIST

Baleen Whales

Family: Balaenidae

1. North Atlantic right whale *(Eubalaena glacialis)*
2. North Pacific right whale *(Eubalaena japonica)*
3. Southern right whale *(Eubalaena australis)*
4. Bowhead whale *(Balaena mysticetus)*

Family: Neobalaenidae

5. Pygmy right whale *(Caperea marginata)*

Family: Eschrichtiidae

6. Gray whale *(Eschrichtius robustus)*

Family: Balaenopteridae

7. Humpback whale *(Megaptera novaeangliae)*
8. Minke whale *(Balaenoptera acutorostrata)*
9. Antarctic minke whale *(Balaenoptera bonaerensis)*
10. Bryde's whale *(Balaenoptera edeni)*
11. Sei whale *(Balaenoptera borealis)*
12. Fin whale *(Balaenoptera physalus)*
13. Blue whale *(Balaenoptera musculus)*

Toothed Whales

Family: Physeteridae

14. Sperm whale *(Physeter catodon)*

Family: Kogiidae

15. Pygmy sperm whale *(Kogia breviceps)*
16. Dwarf sperm whale *(Kogia sima)*

Family: Monodontidae

17. Narwhal *(Monodon monoceros)*
18. Beluga *(Delphinapterus leucas)*

Family: Ziphiidae

19. Arnoux's beaked whale *(Berardius arnuxii)*
20. Baird's beaked whale *(Berardius bairdii)*
21. Tropical bottlenose whale *(Indopacetus pacificus)*
22. Shepherd's beaked whale *(Tasmacetus shepherdi)*
23. Cuvier's beaked whale *(Ziphius cavirostris)*
24. Northern bottlenose whale *(Hyperoodon ampullatus)*
25. Southern bottlenose whale *(Hyperoodon planifrons)*
26. Pygmy beaked whale *(Mesoplodon peruvianus)*
27. Spade-toothed whale *(Mesoplodon traversii)*
28. Sowerby's beaked whale *(Mesoplodon bidens)*
29. Andrews' beaked whale *(Mesoplodon bowdoini)*
30. Hubbs' beaked whale *(Mesoplodon carlhubbsi)*
31. Blainville's beaked whale *(Mesoplodon densirostris)*
32. Gervais' beaked whale *(Mesoplodon europaeus)*
33. Ginkgo-toothed beaked whale *(Mesoplodon ginkgodens)*

34.   Gray's beaked whale (*Mesoplodon grayi*)
35.   Hector's beaked whale (*Mesoplodon hectori*)
36.   Strap-toothed whale (*Mesoplodon layardii*)
37.   True's beaked whale (*Mesoplodon mirus*)
38.   Stejneger's beaked whale (*Mesoplodon stejnegeri*)
39.   Perrin's beaked whale (*Mesoplodon perrini*)

Family: Delphinidae

40.   Pygmy killer whale (*Feresa attenuata*)
41.   False killer whale (*Pseudorca crassidens*)
42.   Melon-headed whale (*Peponocephala electra*)
43.   Long-finned pilot whale (*Globicephala melas*)
44.   Short-finned pilot whale (*Globicephala macrorhynchus*)
45.   Killer whale (*Orcinus orca*)

46.   Risso's dolphin (*Grampus griseus*)
47.   Irrawaddy dolphin (*Orcaella brevirostris*)
48.   Tucuxi (*Sotalia fluviatilis*)
49.   Spinner dolphin (*Stenella longirostris*)
50.   Clymene dolphin (*Stenella clymene*)
51.   Striped dolphin (*Stenella coeruleoalba*)
52.   Pantropical spotted dolphin (*Stenella attenuata*)
53.   Atlantic spotted dolphin (*Stenella frontalis*)
54.   Atlantic hump-backed dolphin (*Sousa teuszii*)
55.   Indo-Pacific hump-backed dolphin (*Sousa chinensis*)
56.   Northern rightwhale dolphin (*Lissodelphis borealis*)
57.   Southern rightwhale dolphin (*Lissodelphis peronii*)
58.   Long-beaked common dolphin (*Delphinus capensis*)
59.   Short-beaked common dolphin (*Delphinus delphis*)
60.   Rough-toothed dolphin (*Steno bredanensis*)
61.   Fraser's dolphin (*Lagenodelphis hosei*)
62.   Common bottlenose dolphin (*Tursiops truncatus*)
63.   Indo-Pacific bottlenose dolphin (*Tursiops aduncus*)
64.   Commerson's dolphin (*Cephalorhynchus commersonii*)
65.   Hector's dolphin (*Cephalorhynchus hectori*)

66.   Heaviside's dolphin (*Cephalorhynchus heavisidii*)
67.   Chilean dolphin (*Cephalorhynchus eutropia*)
68.   Hourglass dolphin (*Lagenorhynchus cruciger*)
69.   Peale's dolphin (*Lagenorhynchus australis*)
70.   Dusky dolphin (*Lagenorhynchus obscurus*)
71.   Atlantic white-sided dolphin (*Lagenorhynchus acutus*)
72.   Pacific white-sided dolphin (*Lagenorhynchus obliquidens*)
73.   White-beaked dolphin (*Lagenorhynchus albirostris*)

Family: Iniidae

74.   Amazon river dolphin (*Inia geoffrensis*)

Family: Lipotidae

75.   Baiji (*Lipotes vexillifer*)

Family: Pontoporiidae

76.   Franciscana (*Pontoporia blainvillei*)

Family: Platanistidae

77.   Indus river dolphin (*Platanista minor*)
78.   Ganges river dolphin (*Platanista gangetica*)

Family: Phocoenidae

79.   Vaquita (*Phocoena sinus*)
80.   Harbor porpoise (*Phocoena phocoena*)
81.   Burmeister's porpoise (*Phocoena spinipinnis*)
82.   Spectacled porpoise (*Phocoena dioptrica*)
83.   Finless porpoise (*Neophocaena phocaenoides*)
84.   Dall's porpoise (*Phocoenoides dalli*)

GLOSSARY

Amphipod—small, shrimplike crustacean that is a food source for some whales.

Baleen/baleen plates—comblike plates hanging down from the upper jaws of most large whales; used instead of teeth to capture prey.

Baleen whale—suborder of whales with baleen plates instead of teeth, known in the scientific world as Mysticeti.

Beak—elongated snout of many cetaceans.

Blow—cloud of water vapor exhaled by cetaceans (also known as the spout); often used to describe the act of breathing.

Blowhole(s)—nasal opening(s) or nostril(s) on the top of the head.

Blubber—layer of fat just beneath the skin of marine mammals; important for insulation instead of fur.

Bow-riding—riding in the pressure wave in front of a boat, ship, or big whale.

Breaching—leaping completely (or almost completely) out of the water, and landing back with a splash.

Bubble-netting—feeding technique used by humpback whales in which they produce fishing nets by blowing bubbles underwater.

Callosity—area of roughened skin on the head of a right whale, to which whale lice and barnacles attach themselves.

Cetacean—any member of the order Cetacea, which includes all whales, dolphins, and porpoises.

Copepod—a small crustacean that is a food source for some whales.

Crustacean—member of a class of invertebrates (animals without backbones) that is a food source for many marine animals; mostly aquatic.

Dorsal fin—raised structure on the back of most (but not all) cetaceans; not supported by bone.

Drift net—fishing net that hangs in the water, unseen and undetectable, and is carried freely with the ocean currents and winds; strongly criticized for catching everything in its path, from seabirds and turtles to whales and dolphins.

Echolocation—process of sending out sounds and interpreting the returning echoes to build up a "sound picture," as in sonar; used by many cetaceans to orientate themselves, navigate, and find food.

Flipper—flattened, paddle-shaped limb of a marine mammal; refers to the front limb of a cetacean (also known as the pectoral fin).

Flipper-slapping—raising a flipper out of the water and slapping it onto the surface.

Fluke—horizontally flattened tail of a cetacean; contains no bone.

Fluking—raising the tail flukes into the air upon diving.

Gill net—similar to a drift net in design, although much smaller and fixed in one position near the coast or in a river.

Hydrophone—waterproofed, underwater microphone.

Keel—distinctive bulge on the tail stock near the flukes.

Krill—small, shrimplike crustaceans that form the major food of many large whales; there are about 80 different species, ranging from $\frac{1}{3}$ inch to just over two inches in length.

Lobtailing—slapping tail flukes against the water, creating a splash.

Logging—lying still at or near the surface.

Mandible—lower jaw of the skull.

Melon—fatty organ in the bulging forehead of many toothed cetaceans, believed to be used to focus sounds for echolocation.

Pectoral fin—see flipper.

Photo-identification—technique for studying cetaceans using photographs as a permanent record of identifiable individuals.

Pod—coordinated group of whales; normally used for larger, toothed whales.

Polar—region around either the North Pole or South Pole (i.e. the Arctic or Antarctic).

Porpoising—leaping out of the water while swimming at speed.

Purse-seine net—long net set around a shoal of fish, then gathered at the bottom and drawn in to form a purse.

Rorqual—baleen whale of the genus *Balaenoptera*; many experts also include the humpback whale (genus *Megaptera*) in this group.

Rostrum—upper jaw of the skull (may be used to refer to the beak or snout).

School—coordinated group of cetaceans; term normally used in association with dolphins.

Snout—see beak.

Sonar—see echolocation.

Spout—see blow.

Spyhopping—raising the head vertically out of the water, apparently to look around above the surface.

Submarine canyon—deep, steep-sided valley in the continental shelf.

Tail stock—muscular region of the tail between the flukes and the dorsal fin.

Temperate—midlatitude regions between the tropics and the poles.

Toothed whale—suborder of whales with teeth, known in the scientific world as Odontoceti.

Tropical—low-latitude regions of the world between the tropics of Capricorn   and Cancer.

Tubercle—circular bumps found on some cetaceans; usually along the edges of flippers and dorsal fins, but also on a humpback whale's head.

Turbid—muddy or cloudy water carrying lots of sediment.

Wake-riding—swimming in the frothy wake of a boat or ship.

Whalebone—another name for baleen.

FURTHER READING

There are far too many excellent books on whales, dolphins, and porpoises to list them all. But here is a small and varied selection:

Carwardine, Mark, Hoyt, Erich, Fordyce, R. Ewan, and Gill, Peter, *Whales & Dolphins: The Ultimate Guide to Marine Mammals*, HarperCollins, 1998.

Darling, James D., Nicklin, Charles Flip, Norris, Kenneth S., Whitehead, Hal and Warsig, Bernd, *Whales, Dolphins, and Porpoises*, National Geographic Society, Washington, 1995.

Ford, John K.B., Ellis, Graeme M., and Balcomb, Kenneth C., *Killer Whales*, UBC Press, 2000.

Hoyt, Erich, *Marine Protected Areas For Whales, Dolphins, and Porpoises*, Earthscan, 2005.

Katona, Steven and Lien, Jon, *A Guide to the Photographic Identification of Individual Whales*, American Cetacean Society, 1990.

Leatherwood, Stephen and Reeves, Randall R., *The Sierra Club Handbook of Whales and Dolphins*, Sierra Club Books, 1983.

Mann, J., Connor, R.C., Tyack, P.L., and Whitehead, H. (eds), *Cetacean Societies: Field Studies of Dolphins and Whales*, University of Chicago Press, 2000.

Payne, Stefani, *Arctic Whales*, Greystone Books, 1995.

Perrin, William F., Wursig, Bernd, and Thewissen, J.G.M. (eds.), *Encyclopedia of Marine Mammals*, Academic Press, 2002.

Reeves, Randall R., Stewart, Brent S., Clapham, Phillip J., Powell, James A., and Folkens, Pieter, A., *Sea Mammals of the World*, A & C Black, 2002.

Reeves, R.R., Smith, B.D., Crespo, E.A., Notarbartolo di Sciara, G., *Dolphins, Whales, and Porpoises: 2002–2010 Conservation Action Plan for the World's Cetaceans*, IUCN, 2002.

Simmonds, Mark P. and Hutchinson, Judith D. (eds.), *The Conservation of Whales and Dolphins: Science and Practice*, J. Wiley, 1996.

Simmonds, Mark, *Whales and Dolphins of the World*, New Holland, 2004.

Waller, Geoffrey (ed.), *Sealife: A Complete Guide to the Marine Environment*,   Pica Press, 1996.

Whitehead, H., *Sperm Whales: Social Evolution in the Ocean*, University of Chicago Press, 2003.

WorldLife Library (various authors), *Blue Whales; Minke Whales; Humpback Whales; Gray Whales; Sperm Whales; Right Whales; Killer Whales; Beluga Whales; Bottlenose Dolphins; Porpoises*; Colin Baxter, 1994-2004.

INDEX

WHAT NEXT?

For more information about whales and dolphins or to learn about places you can go to see them in the wild, contact the American Cetacean Society (www.acsonline.org). They offer whale-watching trips with certified naturalists throughout the year. These trips are excellent educational opportunites and act as fundraisers to help the society's education and conservation programs. You can obtain details on dates and prices by visiting their website, writing to ACS Whale Adventures, P.O. Box 1391, San Pedro CA 90733-1391, or calling their Special Trips Line on (310) 548-7821.

If you would like to see whales and dolphins in captivity but want to be sure to support aquariums that work toward putting the welfare of their mammals first, the American Zoo and Aquarium Association (www.aza.org) can provide you with a list of AZA accredited zoos and aquariums. The AZA, founded in 1924, is dedicated to the advancement of zoos and aquariums in the areas of conservation, education, and science and envisions a world where people respect, value, and conserve animals. Their mailing address is 8403 Colesville Road, Suite 710, Silver Spring MD 20910-3314 or you can telephone them on (301) 562 0777.

Contact the National Audubon Society (www.audubon.org) if you are concerned about conserving whales and dolphins. As well as offering information, it keeps track of current government policy, and can tell you how to get involved and make your views known. It runs conservation campaigns, including one called Living Oceans. You can also write to the society at 700 Broadway, New York, NY 10003 or telephone (212) 979 3000.

The Marine Mammal Center (www.tmmc.org) rescues, rehabilitates, and releases marine wildlife, as well as running education programs and undertaking research. You can find out how to volunteer to work with this organization by visiting their website or writing to them at Marin Headlands, 1065 Fort Cronkhite, Sausalito, CA, 95445. The Wildlife Conservation Society (www.wcs.org) saves wildlife. Their website has features about marine conservation efforts worldwide. Contact them on their website.